MILESTONES
IN MODERN
WORLD HISTORY

The Cuban
Revolution

MILESTONES
IN MODERN
WORLD HISTORY

The Boer War

The Bolshevik
Revolution

The British
Industrial Revolution

The Chinese
Cultural Revolution

The Collapse of
the Soviet Union

The Congress of Vienna

The Cuban Revolution

D-Day and the
Liberation of France

The End of Apartheid
in South Africa

The Establishment
of the State of Israel

The French Revolution
and the Rise
of Napoleon

The Great Irish Famine

The Indian
Independence
Act of 1947

The Iranian Revolution

The Manhattan Project

The Marshall Plan

The Mexican
Revolution

The Treaty of Nanking

The Treaty of Versailles

The Universal
Declaration of
Human Rights

MILESTONES
IN MODERN
WORLD HISTORY

The Cuban Revolution

G.S. PRENTZAS

CHELSEA HOUSE
An Infobase Learning Company

The Cuban Revolution

Chelsea House
An imprint of Infobase Learning
132 West 31st Street
New York, NY 10001

Library of Congress Cataloging-in-Publication Data

Prentzas, G.S.
The Cuban revolution / by G.S. Prentzas.
   p.   cm. — (Milestones in modern world history)
Includes bibliographical references and index.
ISBN 978-1-60413-921-1 (hardcover)
1. Cuba—History—1959–1990—Juvenile literature. 2. Cuba—History—1990–
—Juvenile literature. 3. Cuba—History—Revolution, 1959—Juvenile literature. 4. Castro,
Fidel, 1926–   —Juvenile literature. I. Title. II. Series.
F1788.P74 2011
972.9106'4—dc22   2011004488

Chelsea House books are available at special discounts when purchased in bulk quantities for businesses, associations, institutions, or sales promotions. Please call our Special Sales Department in New York at (212) 967-8800 or (800) 322-8755.

You can find Chelsea House on the World Wide Web at http://www.infobaselearning.com.

Text design by Erik Lindstrom
Cover design by Alicia Post
Composition by Keith Trego
Cover printed by Yurchak Printing, Landisville, Pa.
Book printed and bound by Yurchak Printing, Landisville, Pa.
Date printed: October 2011
Printed in the United States of America

10 9 8 7 6 5 4 3 2 1

This book is printed on acid-free paper.

All links and Web addresses were checked and verified to be correct at the time of publication. Because of the dynamic nature of the Web, some addresses and links may have changed since publication and may no longer be valid.

CONTENTS

The Revolution Begins

In the predawn darkness of January 1, 1959, an airplane lifted off from an airstrip at Camp Columbia, a military base located on the outskirts of Havana, Cuba. Aboard the aircraft were Fulgencio Batista y Zaldívar and members of his family. Hours earlier, Batista had resigned as president of Cuba. He had decided to step down when he heard from his military commanders that Cuba's demoralized army could no longer prevent revolutionaries from seizing Santa Clara, a key town in central Cuba. Before departing, Batista named Supreme Court Justice Carlos Modesto Piedra as Cuba's new president. He also handed over command of the military to General Eulogio Cantillo.

Forty of Batista's closest friends and aides accompanied him on the flight. The pilot steered the aircraft east toward the Dominican Republic. The government of the nearby Caribbean nation had agreed to provide a temporary safe haven for Batista and his associates. A few days later, Batista would admit to journalists that the battle against rebels seeking to overthrow his government had been lost. He would insist that he had stepped down because he wanted to end the bloodshed that had wrecked his country. He wished peace and harmony for Cuba. Rebel groups would scoff at Batista's claim, asserting that the disgraced dictator had fled to save his life.

THE REBELS TAKE CONTROL

As word spread that Batista had left the country, Cubans spilled out onto the streets. They sang, danced, and honked car horns to celebrate the end of the brutal, seven-year Batista regime. Since gaining its independence in 1902, Cuba had been plagued by public corruption, governmental incompetence, and political violence. Many Cubans believed that the Batista government's policies mostly benefited wealthy, politically well-connected families and foreign companies.

To contend with the revolutionaries fighting against it, the Batista government eliminated many basic rights, including freedom of the press and freedom of assembly. In its efforts to identify and arrest rebels, Batista's secret police force harassed, tortured, or imprisoned many innocent people. Support for the efforts to topple Batista grew as the revolutionaries began to win the war. A wide range of citizens—from poor farmers and laborers to wealthy businessmen—started providing rebel groups with assistance and financial backing. Many Cubans simply hoped for a quick end to the war and a fresh start for their country.

In Havana, the celebration soon turned ugly. Some people aimed their years of anger and frustration at symbols of the Batista regime. They smashed parking meters, which were owned by Batista's brother-in-law. They vandalized casinos, shattering windows and dragging gambling equipment into the street to set it afire. A truckload of pigs was set free inside one casino. U.S.-organized crime leaders, such as Meyer Lansky, owned many of the casinos. To safeguard their businesses, the mobsters had supported the Batista government with bribes and other payments and Cubans knew that Batista was connected to these places. Looters also broke into stores and the homes of known Batista supporters, walking off with merchandise and private possessions.

Amid this mayhem, rebel groups quickly took control of the capital city. They exchanged gunfire with police officers and soldiers still loyal to the Batista government. Sensing that the military had little public support, most high-ranking army officers had returned to their homes or gone into hiding. Encountering little resistance, members of the Directorio Revolucionario Estudiantil ("Student Revolutionary Directorate") occupied the Presidential Palace. Two brigades of the chief rebel group, the Movimiento 26 de Julio ("26th of July Movement," or M-26-7 for short), easily seized two key military sites in Havana. (The group had been named after a July 26, 1953, rebel raid on a military base.) On January 2, 1959, one M-26-7 brigade, under the leadership of Camilo Cienfuegos, took control of Camp Columbia. It was Cuba's principal military base, built by the U.S. government after the Spanish-American War of 1898. The other M-26-7 brigade, under the leadership of Argentine revolutionary Che Guevara, arrived in Havana during the early morning hours of January 3. His fighters occupied La Cabaña, an imposing fort overlooking the entrance to Havana's harbor. As the M-26-7 rebels slowly began to restore order in Havana, the country's best-known rebel leader remained hundreds of miles away in eastern Cuba.

FIDEL CASTRO

The leader of the entire M-26-7 movement, Fidel Castro, was eating breakfast in a rural area of Oriente Province on New Year's Day when he heard from a journalist that Batista had fled the country. A former lawyer, Castro had masterminded and

(continues on page 13)

FIDEL CASTRO:
A TIRELESS REVOLUTIONARY

Born on August 13, 1926, Fidel Castro Ruz grew up in the Oriente Province in eastern Cuba. (Like most people of Spanish or Latino ancestry, Castro has two last names; his father's, Castro, and his mother's, Ruz. In American usage, typically only the father's name is used for identification.) His family owned a sugarcane plantation and was relatively wealthy. Castro attended elite Catholic schools in Santiago and Havana before entering the University of Havana Law School in 1945, where he became friends with students who wanted a truly democratic Cuba, free from the powerful American influence on their nation's government and economy. Castro became politically active, participating in strikes and demonstrations against the Cuban government. After graduating, he set up a law practice in Havana, where he often represented poor clients for free. Politics, however, excited Castro more than the law; in 1952, he ran for a seat in Cuba's legislature. The election was canceled, however, when Fulgencio Batista gained control of the government following a military coup.

Concluding that reforming the government through elections and other democratic processes had become impossible, Castro decided to join the budding revolution against Batista's regime. In the summer of 1953, he led a disastrous raid on a military base in Santiago. Nearly all of the rebels were killed or imprisoned. Castro served nearly 2 years of a 15-year sentence at the dreaded Isla de Pinos ("Isle of Pines") prison before being released in 1955.

Castro rejoined surviving members of his rebel group, now known as the 26th of July Movement (M-26-7), in

Mexico. There, the M-26-7 reorganized and recruited new members. Before returning to their homeland in late 1956, they received training in conducting ambushes, raids, and other methods of guerrilla, or unconventional, warfare. (*Guerrilla* is a Spanish word meaning "little war.") From its hideouts in the Sierra Maestra Mountains in southeastern Cuba, the M-26-7 planned and launched repeated guerrilla attacks against the Batista government. Month by month, Castro slowly transformed from the commander of a tiny, ragtag band of rebels to the leader of a powerful revolutionary movement that was gaining control of Cuba. A series of rebel victories by the M-26-7 and other revolutionary groups prompted Batista to flee the country on New Year's Day, 1959.

Castro soon assumed the position of prime minister, taking control of Cuba's government, military, and economy. Cuba's 1960 seizure of properties and businesses owned by U.S. citizens and companies—along with a failed U.S.-backed invasion to overthrow the Castro government the following year—soured the relationship between the two countries. The tensions grew in 1962 when Cuba strengthened its ties with the Soviet Union. The Soviets began to build missile pads in Cuba, resulting in the Cuban Missile Crisis. Castro had thrust his country into the middle of a dangerous confrontation between two superpowers. Until the Soviets began dismantling the missile pads, the world teetered on the brink of a nuclear war.

The Cuban leader soon became identified with his defiance toward the United States and his ruthlessness in advancing the Cuban Revolution. To some, Castro was a celebrated champion of the poor who stood up to the powerful United States and introduced social justice and equality to his country. The charismatic revolutionary

(continues)

(continued)

inspired fellow Cubans and oppressed people throughout Latin America and the world. To others, he was a despised dictator who trampled democratic ideals, forced many Cubans to leave their country, and adopted the same repressive measures used by the Batista regime that he had overthrown.

Over the next five decades, Castro ruled Cuba with an iron fist. A complex, contradictory personality, his only loyalty appeared to be to the Cuban Revolution. He refused to tolerate those "who have no stomach for a strong revolution."* He abandoned—and sometimes imprisoned—longtime friends and fellow revolutionaries who disagreed with his views. He adopted increasingly harsh and extreme policies, certain that they would move the ideals of the Cuban Revolution forward.

Several unsuccessful assassination attempts convinced Castro that he had enemies everywhere, within the country and abroad. After years of declining health, Castro became seriously ill in 2006 and transferred control of the government to his brother Raúl. His disappearance from public view fueled speculation that he was nearing death. Castro's supporters and his critics began wondering about the future of Cuba without Fidel. In 2009, however, Castro reappeared, making appearances at several official events. At age 83, he looked healthy and robust. The level of his participation in Cuba's government, however, remained uncertain.

In April 2011, Fidel Castro stepped down as first secretary of the Cuban Communist Party and was replaced by his brother, Raúl.

---

* Tad Szulc, "Clues to the Enigma Called Castro," *New York Times Magazine*, December 9, 1962, p. 93.

(continued from page 9)
led the 1953 surprise attack against more than 1,000 of Batista's troops. The reckless, poorly planned mission had failed miserably. During the clash, government troops killed more than 60 rebels and eventually captured about 40 others, including Castro and his brother Raúl. For his role in the plot, Castro had been sentenced to 15 years in prison. The Batista government released him nearly two years later, when it pardoned many political prisoners. After an 18-month exile in Mexico, Fidel Castro returned to Cuba in 1956 to resume the revolt against the Batista government.

Realizing that Batista's sudden departure might allow military leaders—or other, more moderate rebel groups—to seize power, Castro ordered Cienfuegos and Guevara to rush their fighters to Havana. By 11 A.M., he had found a rural radio station and broadcast a speech that denounced the appointments of Modesto and Cantillo. The rebel leader asserted that the two men would continue the policies of the Batista government. To paralyze any efforts to set up a new military-led government, Castro asked Cubans to stop working, shopping, and going about their daily business. The general strike would also discourage looting and, by keeping citizens off of the streets, enable his rebel forces to gain control of Havana more easily. "After seven years of struggle," he concluded, "the democratic victory of the people has to be absolute, so that never again will there be in our country another 10th of March."[1] (Batista had seized control of Cuba's government by leading a successful military takeover on March 10, 1952.) Radio stations across the island rebroadcast Castro's speech.

Few Cubans wanted yet another government controlled by the army. In a view shared by the rebels and many others, Castro believed that revolution had been the only way to oust Batista and to form a government that would benefit all Cubans. At age 32, he was confident that he was ready to lead his country toward its new destiny.

After the radio speech, Castro and his group of fighters sped toward Santiago de Cuba, the capital of Oriente Province. Santiago was the nation's second-largest city and its most important seaport. After seizing control of the city, Castro made a speech from a balcony overlooking Santiago's Parque Céspedes on January 2, 1959. He announced the formation of a provisional (temporary) government. Respected by the liberal cause, former judge Manuel Urrutia would serve as president. Castro himself would serve as commander of the nation's armed forces. Elections would be held in the near future.

Castro pledged that Cuba would, at long last, have an honest, democratic government. He also vowed that the new government would be independent of its powerful neighbor, the United States. He declared, "The Revolution begins now. This time will not be like 1898 when the North Americans came and made themselves masters of our country. This time, fortunately, the Revolution will truly come to power."[2] Despite the speech's anti-American language, Castro had a friendly dinner with a U.S. diplomat in Santiago that night.

THE VICTORY MARCH

Leaving his brother Raúl in charge of Santiago, Castro prepared to make his way to Havana. On January 3, Castro and about 300 rebels set out on a slow, triumphant journey across the island. Enthusiastic crowds stretched along the main highway to cheer them. Television crews followed Castro's entourage, providing Cubans with up-to-the-minute reports on the victory march. Castro met with rebel commanders and local politicians. He granted interviews to foreign journalists, giving the world a closer look at the self-assured rebel leader.

Along the way, more and more rebels joined the procession. The expanding motorcade of tanks, jeeps, trucks, and cars stopped in several towns so Castro could make speeches. In Camagüey Province, it took Castro, sitting atop a tank, nearly three hours to inch his way through an excited crowd of more

The Cuban rebel leader Fidel Castro (*center right*) waves during a large rally in front of the Presidential Palace in Havana, Cuba, in January 1959. More than a million people jammed every inch of space around the palace to see the young rebel who had overthrown the hated Batista regime.

than 100,000 people. Describing the jubilant scene, a *New York Times* reporter wrote, "Once he was a hunted man with a small band of followers, but today he is the hero of all Cuba."[3]

While in Camagüey, Castro made a speech asking Cubans to end the strike and resume their usual activities. The widespread public embrace of the strike had quickly convinced military leaders and Batista supporters that they should not oppose Castro. He also vowed to reorganize the armed forces. The military would now be "exclusively at the service of the Cuban people" and a "model institution," Castro declared.[4]

In Havana, M-26-7 rebels quickly earned the trust of the city residents and foreign visitors. Although the scruffy, bearded, gun-toting fighters appeared intimidating, they were well organized and reserved. They guarded government buildings and prevented looting. They treated citizens respectfully. The M-26-7 soon gained the upper hand in Havana. It pressured the Directorio Revolucionario to hand over control of the Presidential Palace before President Urrutia arrived in Havana. M-26-7 rebels also began rounding up high-ranking officials of the Batista government and military.

Hundreds of thousands of people greeted Castro's motorcade when it reached Havana on the afternoon of January 8. They lined the streets, waving flags, flinging confetti at the victorious rebels, and holding signs that read "Gracias Fidel." Wearing his trademark khaki fatigues and clutching a rifle, Castro rode into Havana in a jeep. More than 5,000 armed rebels marched behind him in columns. Castro stopped at the Presidential Palace to meet with Urrutia, his cabinet, and other supporters of the revolution. Having had little sleep over the past week, the tired revolutionary spoke briefly to the overjoyed masses. He invited all Cubans to Camp Columbia that evening. He would give a more formal speech then.

That night, more than 10,000 people jammed the parade grounds at Camp Columbia. In a passionate two-hour speech, Castro promised to lead Cuba into a new age of freedom, democracy, and good government. He promised "a peace without dictatorship, without crimes, without censorship, and without deceptions."[5] He warned his listeners that building a new

This photograph was taken in 1957 during the guerrilla war against the Batista regime. Seen here are rebel leaders Che Guevara (top, second from left) and Fidel Castro (top, second from right). Kneeling in the foreground is Raúl Castro, brother of Fidel.

Cuba would require much effort: "This is a decisive moment in our history: The tyranny has been overthrown, but there is still much to be done. Let us not fool ourselves into believing that the future will be easy; perhaps everything will be more difficult in the future."[6]

Ruby Hart Phillips, a *New York Times* reporter who attended the speech, would later write, "As I watched Castro, I realized the magic of his personality. . . . He seemed to weave a hypnotic web over his listeners, making them believe in his own concept of the functions of Government and the destiny of Cuba."[7]

Castro continued speaking, appealing for unity among the various revolutionary groups. In an obvious ploy to strengthen his own power, he called for all rebel fighters to put down their weapons. "No private armies will be tolerated," he cautioned.[8] He assured military officers and soldiers that most of them would keep their posts. "Those who have committed crimes," Castro vowed, "will face a firing squad."[9]

Earlier in the speech, someone in the crowd had released three doves. One flew directly to Castro and perched on his shoulder as he spoke. Long considered a symbol of peace and love, the dove seemed to herald a bright future for Cubans and their country.

Origins of the
Cuban Revolution

L ocated in the Caribbean Sea, the country of Cuba consists of a large island (Cuba), the Isla de la Juventud ("Isle of Youth," which was called the Isla de Pinos before 1978), and more than 1,600 small islands. It is the largest and western-most island of the Greater Antilles, a chain of four large islands in the Caribbean Sea. The country has a total land mass of 42,402 square miles (109,820 sq km), making it slightly smaller than Pennsylvania.

Located 90 miles (145 km) south of Key West, Florida, and 130 miles (209 km) east of Mexico's Yucatan Peninsula, Cuba has long occupied a strategic spot in the Caribbean. Situated where the Atlantic Ocean, Caribbean Sea, and the Gulf of Mexico meet, it became a key colonial possession of Spain during the sixteenth century. As European nations fought for control of the Americas, Cuba grew into an important military base and a busy trading center. It soon became known as the "Pearl of the Antilles." After gaining its independence from Spain at the end of the nineteenth century, Cuba experienced much political turmoil and violence, all of which would lead to the Cuban Revolution.

THE EARLIEST CUBANS

The Siboney (or Ciboney) people were the earliest human inhabitants of present-day Cuba. Originally from what is now Venezuela, they traveled west by boat and settled on islands throughout the Caribbean. The Siboney first arrived in Cuba in about 1000 B.C. They made their homes in caves, primarily on the western and southern coasts of Cuba. (*Siboney* is the Arawak Indian word meaning "cave dweller.") Little is known about the Siboney because no written record of their history, language, or culture exists.

In the ninth century A.D., the Taíno arrived from the nearby island of Hispaniola. The Taíno were part of a larger group of native peoples known as the Arawak, who lived in northeastern South America and on the islands of the Greater Antilles. The Taíno first settled along the eastern coast of Cuba, then later moved inland, building large villages holding about 2,000 residents. In addition to hunting, fishing, and gathering, they planted corn, tomatoes, yucca, and other vegetables. The Taíno used the yucca's root (similar to a potato) to make cassava bread, an important part of their diet. They also cultivated tobacco, which was used in religious ceremonies.

THE SPANISH ARRIVE

In 1492, Christopher Columbus arrived in the Caribbean. Spanish monarchs Ferdinand and Isabella had hired the Italian navigator to find a western sea route to Asia. In October of that year, Columbus's three ships sailed along the northeastern coast of Cuba, near present-day Baracoa. Columbus came ashore on October 28, 1492. He named the island "Juana" in honor of Juana, Ferdinand and Isabella's daughter. At the time, Cuba was home to about 100,000 Taíno and about 10,000 Siboney. They had several names for the island, including "Cubanacan."

Two years later, Columbus made his second voyage to the Americas. On April 30, 1494, he arrived off the southern coast of Cuba and anchored in the present-day harbor of Guantánamo. In his logbook, he described the Taíno village there as "looking like tents in a camp, without regular streets but one here and there. Within, they were clean & well-swept, with well-made furniture. All were made of palm branches, beautifully constructed."[1]

Columbus's explorations spurred Spanish efforts to colonize the region. Spanish adventurers, later known as conquistadors, sailed west to find gold, silver, and other treasures fabled to be found in what they called "the New World." Early Spanish colonial efforts in the Greater Antilles focused on the island of Hispaniola, where the Spanish established their first permanent settlement in the Western Hemisphere at Santo Domingo in 1498.

Spanish officials and colonists ignored Cuba at first. Too many colonists and not enough money-making opportunities, however, made settlers cast an eye toward Hispaniola's western neighbor. In 1511, conquistador Diego Velázquez de Cuéllar received official orders to settle the island of Cuba. He assembled a group of 300 men and sailed to Cuba, landing at present-day Maisi on the island's eastern tip. A few miles away, he established the first Spanish settlement in Cuba, calling it Nuestra Señora de las Ascuncion de Baracoa ("Our Lady of the Assumption of Baracoa").

Although Columbus had peacefully met with natives during his explorations of Cuba, Velázquez encountered resistance from the Taíno. A Taíno leader, Hatuey, had witnessed a Spanish massacre of his people on Hispaniola. Fleeing his home, he guided a group of Taíno to Cuba in 1503. Under Hatuey's leadership, a small group of Taíno fought against the Spanish invaders. Outnumbered, they used hit-and-run tactics—engaging in small skirmishes before retreating back into the forests—to wage war against the well-armed Spaniards.

In early 1512, Pánfilo de Narváez arrived on Cuba's southern coast from Jamaica. Leading a small expedition, he united his men with Velázquez's forces to battle against the Taíno. Spanish troops eventually captured Hatuey, who was sentenced to execution for leading the native resistance. He was tied to a stake and burned alive on February 2, 1512. Over the next three years, Narváez's army swept through the island. Mounted on horseback and armed with crossbows, the Spaniards eventually subdued the Taíno, killing as many as 3,000 natives. Many of the survivors fled to the mountains or to small offshore islands. For decades to come, small bands of Taínos would emerge from the mountains and attack Spanish settlements.

In 1513, King Ferdinand declared Cuba as his property. Colonists found small deposits of gold in the mountains of Cuba and quickly mined all of the valuable metal. With few remaining prospects for becoming wealthy, many of the gold seekers turned to farming. Needing laborers to work on their new farms, Spanish settlers began to enslave local Indians. Slavery failed, however, because natives either fled or died from diseases. Thousands of Taínos died from diseases such as measles and smallpox because they had never been exposed to them. These diseases—so common in Europe that many

(opposite page) Cuba's longstanding relationship with Spain began with the arrival of explorer Christopher Columbus to the island in 1492. After centuries as a Spanish colony, Cuba won its independence from Spain in December 1898 with the help of the United States. The island was administered by the United States from 1898 to 1902.

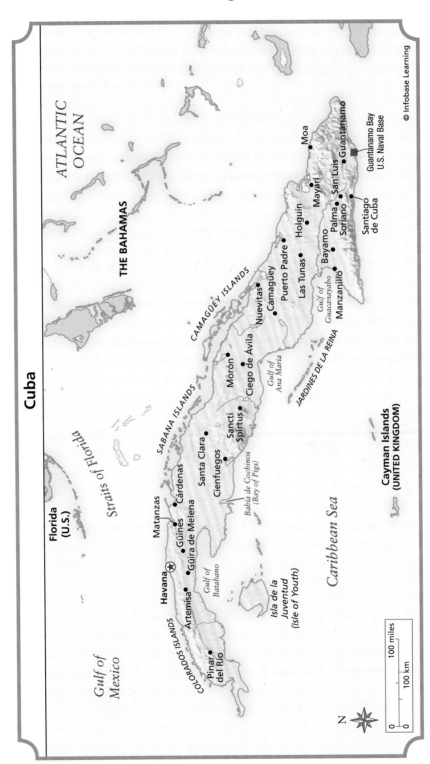

Cuba

ATLANTIC
OCEAN

THE BAHAMAS

Florida
(U.S.)

Straits of Florida

Gulf of
Mexico

COLORADOS ISLANDS

Pinar
del Río

Artemisa

Havana

Güira de Melena

Güines

Matanzas

Cárdenas

Gulf of
Batabanó

Isla de la
Juventud
(Isle of Youth)

SABANA ISLANDS

Santa Clara

Cienfuegos

Sancti
Spíritus

Bahía de Cochinos
(Bay of Pigs)

Morón

Ciego de Ávila

Gulf of
Ana María

CAMAGÜEY ISLANDS

Nuevitas

Camagüey

Puerto Padre

Las Tunas

JARDINES DE LA REINA

Gulf of
Guacanayabo

Manzanillo

Bayamo

Holguín

Mayarí

San Luis

Palma
Soriano

Santiago
de Cuba

Moa

Guantánamo

Guantánamo Bay
U.S. Naval Base

Caribbean Sea

Cayman Islands
(UNITED KINGDOM)

N

0   100 miles
0   100 km

© Infobase Learning

Europeans had built up immunity to them—spread quickly through native populations.

As agricultural development in Cuba progressed slowly, few settlers prospered. Many colonists who became discouraged in Cuba either returned to Spain or moved on to other Spanish colonies in the Americas. The focus of Spanish colonization shifted to Mexico, where the opportunities for making fortunes seemed better. As a result, Spaniards viewed Cuba as a waste of time. Conquistador Hernán Cortés, who later led Spanish forces in their successful campaign to defeat the Aztec Empire, summed up the common attitude toward Cuba: "I came here to get rich, not to till the soil like a peasant."[2]

Many of the colonists who stayed in Cuba married native women. By 1535, Cuba's population included about 300 Spaniards (including children born on the island), 5,000 natives, and 1,000 African slaves. Slavery had been common in southern Spain since the thirteenth century. Many slaves in Spain had been captured in Africa and sold into slavery. The first slaves from Africa had arrived in Cuba in 1522. Unlike the slaves in other parts of the Americas, however, most African slaves in Cuba during this time worked as personal servants rather than as agricultural laborers.

THE AGE OF PIRATES

Although few early Spanish settlers achieved wealth or success in Cuba, they soon recognized the island's greatest natural asset: its deep harbors. The ports that sprang up along these harbors would soon become crucial to the security and prosperity of Spain's colonies in the Americas.

Cuba served as a major hub in Spain's plan for colonial expansion in the Americas. Spanish expeditions launched their invasions to claim and conquer lands in the New World from Cuban ports. Cortés began his offensive against the Aztecs from Havana in 1519. Havana also served as the departing point for the expeditions of Álvar Núñez Cabeza de Vaca (1527) and Hernando de Soto (1539).

By the 1540s, Spain found itself competing with other European countries to establish colonies in the Americas. France, England, and Holland had also begun exploring the New World and sending settlers to colonize newly claimed lands. The European powers hired independent sea captains and their crews, known as pirates or privateers, to prey on their enemy's ships and on New World settlements. Pirates hired by France began attacking Cuban villages and Spanish ships sailing to and from its harbors. In 1555, pirates ransacked Havana, burning it to the ground. While rebuilding the town, Spain erected forts to protect the town's harbor. Havana soon had the strongest defenses against naval attacks in the Americas.

To defend against pirate attacks on ships carrying gold and other treasures from their colonies back to Spain, the Spaniards started transporting their valuables by using convoys of ships to cross the Atlantic Ocean. Because of its large harbor and central location on the eastern edge of the Gulf of Mexico, Havana became the meeting point for Spanish cargo ships. Ships heading back to Spain would dock in Havana and wait there until enough vessels gathered to make a convoy. Accompanied by warships, the cargo ships would then sail together in a large group to Spain. Havana soon became a bustling port city and trading center. Spain enlarged its defenses in Cuba, building forts in all of Cuba's major ports. Despite the presence of Spanish forts and soldiers, Spain's enemies found refuge in remote areas of Cuba. Isla de la Juventud and small, isolated harbors became popular hideouts for pirates.

THE COLONY GROWS

The Spanish Crown appointed a governor to serve as its official representative in Cuba. The governor (later called a captain-general) had complete authority to rule the island as he pleased. The governor and other local officials, however, faced many struggles in managing the growing colony. They had to defend the island and its people against frequent pirate attacks and occasional local raids by natives and escaped slaves. Smugglers presented another threat to the government. To pay for defending the colony and other costs of managing it, the Spanish Crown charged a tax on all goods brought into Cuba. Colonists bristled at the high cost of taxed goods, and smugglers began sneaking untaxed items into the country. Selling illegal goods became a major business on the island. The dangers posed by these pirates, consisting of armed bands of Indians and escaped slaves, and smugglers pushed the governors to rule the island with an iron fist. This tradition of harsh, dictatorial government would endure in Cuba for centuries.

Government officials soon discovered that their control over the island could provide personal enrichment. Smugglers and even pirates bribed colonial officials to ignore various illegal activities. Colonists began to view an appointment to a government post as a way to become wealthy. Colonial officials sold licenses authorizing colonists to conduct certain businesses, such as importing slaves, and pocketed the fees. Some officials even became smugglers themselves.

THE RISE OF SUGAR

Cuba developed close commercial relationships with the nearby islands of Hispaniola and Jamaica, as well as with Spanish settlements in Mexico and Central America. Many colonists became wealthy through trade, both legal and illegal. Government officials, smugglers, and traders were not the only ones getting rich. Other industries on the island began to mature, and the colony's economy was soon based on raising cattle and agriculture. Sugar became the island's major crop.

Because they needed many laborers to harvest and process sugarcane, sugar farmers began to import more African slaves. Slavery in Cuba's agricultural sector expanded under the British, who captured Havana in 1762 and controlled the island for a year. In the 1790s, a slave rebellion in nearby Haiti led to that colony's independence from France. Fleeing the rebellion

This engraving shows a sugar plantation and refinery in Cuba, circa 1683. Sugar production has been a main part of the Cuban economy since its days as a Spanish colony.

and black rule, white Haitian slaveholders moved to Cuba, where they brought their slaves and established large sugar plantations in Oriente, Cuba's easternmost region. The demand for slaves grew as the sugar industry expanded. Between 1762 and 1838, slaveholders imported nearly 400,000 African slaves to Cuba. Slavery would eventually be abolished in 1886.

The sugar industry became central to the colony's economy. Sugar barons amassed large fortunes and dominated Cuba's politics and culture. The growth of Cuba's sugar industry, along with its strategic location, led a new neighbor to show great interest in the island colony. Having gained its independence from England in 1783, the United States began trying to obtain Cuba from Spain. In 1808, President Thomas Jefferson remarked that Cuba was the "key to the Gulf of Mexico."[3] On

KING SUGAR

Blessed with the perfect soil and climate to cultivate sugarcane, Cuba has long been one of the world's leading sugar suppliers. By the mid-1800s, it produced nearly one-third of the world's sugar. The sugar industry soon became the driving force in Cuba's economy. Because cutting sugarcane was such a labor-intensive process, Cuba's earliest sugar plantations were able to produce sugar at low prices by using African slaves. After slavery was abolished in 1886, the sugar plantations paid cane cutters low wages and employed them only during the three-month harvest season.

Wealthy sugar plantation owners soon controlled much of Cuba's society. Throughout the nineteenth century, Spain taxed Cuban sugar to help support its shrinking colonial empire. High taxes and other grievances against the Spanish colonial government sparked Cuban rebellions seeking independence. In the years of political turmoil that followed Cuban independence from Spain in 1898, sugar remained vital to the country's economy. *Sin azucar no hay pais* ("Without sugar there is no country") was a commonly heard phrase in Cuba.

several occasions over the next few decades, the U.S. government offered to buy Cuba, but Spain refused each time.

As the colony grew, it developed into a multiracial society. The island's white residents were mostly Spanish, although some immigrants came from France, Italy, and other European countries. Most white settlers started out as farmers, but they soon controlled most aspects of the island's government and economy. The island's black population was made up of slaves from Africa and free people of color, who worked in cities as laborers or artisans. By 1860, the island's population consisted of 716,000

By the 1950s, sugarcane covered more than half of Cuba's farmlands. The sugar industry employed about one-third of Cuban workers. Sugar accounted for about 30 percent of the nation's total income and more than 90 percent of its export income. During that decade, the United States bought about 3 million tons (2.7 million metric tons) of Cuban sugar each year.

After Fidel Castro came to power in 1959, his government sought to end Cuba's dependency on the sugar industry. It focused its resources on developing the nation's industrial base. When the U.S. government suspended its sugar purchases and ended all trade with Cuba in 1961, the Cuban government again made sugar production a national priority. From the early 1960s until the late 1990s, the Castro government sold sugar to the Soviet Union (later Russia) and its allies at favorable prices. The collapse of the Soviet Union in the late 1980s, however, ended the lucrative deal. In 2002, the Cuban government began downsizing the sugar industry to devote more of its agricultural resources to raising other crops. Although it no longer plays a vital role in the national economy, sugar has an enduring place in Cuban history and culture.

white residents and 643,000 black residents. A small, surviving population of Táinos lived in remote mountain villages.

THE PUSH FOR INDEPENDENCE

Throughout the nineteenth century, Cuba's fortunes were tied to those of Spain. Over the centuries, Spain had weakened as a world power. Its wars against European neighbors and rebellions on Hispaniola and Puerto Rico had stretched its armies. Increasingly, Spain began to rely on Cuba and its sugar industry to support its crumbling empire. As Cubans became increasingly irritated about paying high taxes, murmurings of independence were heard throughout the island.

Cubans made their first attempt at independence in 1868. Carlos Manuel de Céspedes led a group of landowners who seized the town of Bayamo. They signed a declaration of independence, called the Grito de Yara, and their revolt spread to other parts of the island. Spanish troops, however, soon subdued the rebellion; by the next year, they had recovered all of the seized territory. Although underequipped and outmanned, the Cuban rebels continued fighting. Instead of engaging in a conventional war against the better-armed and better-trained Spanish troops, they started a guerrilla war in which they avoided direct confrontations with Spanish soldiers. Instead, they attacked remote military posts and isolated troops and burned sugar plantations of Cubans who supported Spanish colonialism.

Spanish troops showed little mercy. They executed young men merely suspected of supporting the rebels. To isolate and identify rebels, the Spaniards moved rural people into towns. Spanish authorities warned Cubans that anyone found in the countryside would be considered a rebel and executed. Over the next nine years, neither side gained an advantage. The Spaniards managed to limit the rebellion to the eastern region of the island. In western Cuba, life went on as usual.

Spanish authorities grew tired of the rebellion, and internal disputes began to weaken the rebels. In 1878, both sides agreed to a peace plan. Spanish authorities offered amnesty to all rebels and promised to make political reforms. Because many rebels were escaped slaves, the government offered them freedom and promised to outlaw racial discrimination in schools and other areas of Cuban society. The rebels agreed to the plan, but a fresh rebellion broke out in eastern Cuba a year later. Although the Spanish quickly defeated the rebellion, tensions remained high for years. Minor rebellions occasionally broke out, and rumors of rebellion remained constant. To confront the unrest, colonial officials adopted increasingly harsh restrictions. Many of the most vocal opponents to Spanish rule left the island and advocated Cuban independence from abroad.

One of the exiles pushing for Cuban independence was José Martí. Born in Havana in 1853, Martí began supporting Cuban independence as a college student. Imprisoned for his activism, he was exiled to Spain by colonial authorities. Martí later moved to New York, where he founded the Cuban Revolutionary Party in 1892. A journalist and a poet, he soon devoted his life to planning a war to overthrow Spanish rule.

On April 1, 1895, Martí launched his plan. Three groups would invade Cuba and lead a popular uprising against Spanish rule. One group, led by Antonio Maceo Grajales, departed from Costa Rica and landed near Baracoa. U.S. officials, however, stopped the ship transporting the second group before it could reach Cuba. Martí joined the third group, led by Maximo Gómez, which landed near Guantánamo on April 11. The group joined with Maceo's unit and began to fight Spanish troops. On May 19, a Spanish ambush surprised Gómez's group, and Martí was killed in the gun battle. The charismatic Martí would become the hero of Cuban independence and revered by later revolutionary groups.

Despite losing its political and inspirational leader, the rebellion carried on. At first, Spanish troops confined the uprising to the eastern part of the island. This rebellion, however, had much more support than earlier independence movements. Spain sent an additional 16,000 troops to quash it. Led by Gómez and Maceo, the rebels moved into central Cuba in October 1895. They attacked sugar plantations, burning cane fields and sugar mills. They had only a few direct encounters with Spanish troops. Over the next six months, the rebels marched across the island. By early 1896, Gómez pushed forward to the outskirts of Havana as Maceo's troops moved into the Pinar del Río region in western Cuba.

Unhappy with the rebel gains, Spain sent a new captain-general, Valeriano Weyler, to Cuba. He ordered troops to attack the rebels, who had little experience in traditional warfare. Spanish troops on the island, which now numbered 60,000, began pushing the rebels back. To prevent local residents from giving the rebels support, Weyler set up camps and moved rural Cubans into them. He also issued a decree stating that anyone who refused to move to a camp would be guilty of treason and executed. Soldiers herded hundreds of thousands of rural residents into the camps. Suffering from hunger and poor sanitation, many Cubans died in the camps from disease. By the end of 1896, Weyler gained the upper hand. Spanish troops killed Maceo in December and drove Gómez's forces back into eastern Cuba.

As the war for independence in Cuba dragged on, it gained much attention in the United States. U.S. newspapers catalogued the violent measures taken by the Spanish government, focusing especially on the horrible conditions in Weyler's concentration camps. U.S. government officials and the business community wanted Cuba to gain its independence from Spain. Cuban independence would improve U.S. security and provide new economic opportunities for U.S. businesses. In January 1898, the head U.S. diplomat in Havana requested assistance when rioting broke out in the city. The U.S. Navy sent a battleship to Cuba to protect U.S. interests there.

After the USS *Maine* blew up and sank in Havana harbor on February 15, 1898 (with the loss of 258 men), the United States declared war on Spain in April 1898. The U.S. victory in that conflict resulted in the eventual independence of Cuba in 1902.

On February 15, 1898, the U.S. battleship *Maine* exploded and sank in Havana's harbor, killing 258 American sailors. The U.S. press blamed a Spanish mine. Spanish authorities claimed that an internal explosion destroyed the vessel. (A 1970 study produced by U.S. admiral Hyman Rickover concluded that the explosion was prompted by an internal coal fire that broke out next to the ammunition storage area.) When the two sides failed to negotiate a settlement to the incident, the United

States declared war on Spain on April 25, 1898. The Spanish-American War, as it became known, was not confined to Cuba. U.S. forces also attacked Spanish colonies in the Pacific, including the Philippines.

In Cuba, U.S. troops landed at Guantánamo Bay, where they united with rebel forces. On June 22, a landing force of 6,000 U.S. troops came ashore near Santiago. The war's only major land battle was fought on San Juan Hill, near Santiago. On July 1, 3,000 U.S. soldiers attacked a much smaller group of Spanish defenders. As U.S. troops advanced on Santiago, the Spanish fleet steamed out of the city's harbor. The waiting U.S. Navy then sank every Spanish ship.

Cuban rebel leaders had welcomed U.S. intervention and had worked with U.S. troops during the invasion. They thought the war between the United States and Spain would lead to Cuban independence. The war declaration of the U.S. Congress stated that U.S. involvement in Cuba would be temporary. When the United States and Spain negotiated a peace treaty in Paris, however, no Cubans were invited. Spain transferred possession of Cuba, Puerto Rico, and its Pacific colonies of Guam and the Philippines to the United States. The Spanish-American War destroyed the last remaining parts of Spain's once-powerful empire, which had lasted for more than 400 years.

THE CUBAN REPUBLIC

After the war ended, the U.S. government ruled Cuba for more than three years. In December 1898, President McKinley told the U.S. Congress that the United States would remain in Cuba "[u]ntil there is complete tranquility in the island and a stable government inaugurated."[4] The United States appointed General Leonard Wood as military governor to oversee the island. Having expected that their struggle against Spain would result in independence, Cubans gave Wood little assistance. When the United States officially annexed Puerto Rico, many Cubans assumed that their island would also become a permanent U.S. territory.

As delegates began to draft Cuba's first constitution in 1900, U.S. officials offered them a deal. If they agreed to include certain terms in the constitution, the United States would end its occupation. The United States wanted the right to "intervene for the preservation of Cuban independence" and the right to a set up a permanent naval base in Guantánamo Bay.[5] It also wanted the power to oversee public finances and wanted Cuba to agree not to sign any treaty with another country without U.S. approval. By a 16–11 vote, the delegates voted to include the U.S. terms into Cuba's constitution. Those voting in favor reasoned that these less-than-desirable terms were better than continued U.S. occupation. The Platt Amendment, as the agreement would become known, would stay in force until 1934. Its terms would hinder the development of Cuban political institutions and complicate the relationship between Cuba and the United States.

Cuba held its first election under the new constitution in 1901. All Cuban males 20 years old or older who could read and write and owned property valued at $250 or more were qualified to vote. Voters elected Tómas Estrada Palma as the nation's first president. The political parties that advocated Cuban independence defeated the U.S.-backed party that supported U.S. annexation. The United States complied with the voters' wishes and transferred control of Cuba to Estrada's government on May 20, 1902.

Although Cuba experienced dramatic economic growth during Estrada's presidency, political corruption plagued his term. Many Cuban officials, accustomed to the dishonest practices of the Spanish colonial government, used their positions in the new government for personal gain. Estrada was reelected in 1906, but political opponents charged that widespread fraud invalidated the election results. Opposition forces, led by losing presidential candidate José Miguel Gómez, began an armed insurrection. As Gómez's rebels marched toward Havana, Estrada asked the United States for assistance. Because Cuba had yet to organize an army, President Theodore Roosevelt dispatched U.S. Marine units to Cuba. Estrada and his cabinet resigned, and U.S. officials took charge. Over the next two years, they trained a small army and set up a more reliable system of voting.

Gómez won the 1908 presidential election and ruled until 1913. Over the next 12 years, political instability increased as charges of election fraud and corruption weakened Cuba's government. The United States sent troops to Cuba twice: in 1912 to defuse a protest by black Cubans against racial discrimination and in 1916 to quell another armed rebellion following an election. To prevent violence and to protect sugar plantations and other American interests, the Marines stayed in Cuba until 1922.

After Gerardo Machado y Morales won the 1924 presidential election, he created an authoritarian government and extended his term in office by cancelling elections in 1928. Following the U.S. stock market crash in 1929, the Cuban economy suffered. Sugar production plunged, leading to massive unemployment and increasing public displeasure with Machado. When students at the University of Havana created an organization to protest against the government, Machado banned it. The students then started a small-scale rebellion, engaging in terrorist attacks and assassination attempts targeting government officials. The students and opposition groups started a general strike against the government in July 1933. Unable to overcome the nation's economic problems and the loss of U.S. support of his administration, Machado resigned on August 12, 1933, and left the country.

Backed by the U.S. government, Carlos Manuel de Céspedes, the son of the Cuban independence leader, was appointed as the new president when Machado stepped down. Opposition rebels, however, continued to fight in rural areas, seizing sugar mills. Discontent in the Cuban military over the ineffectiveness of Céspedes's government soon led a small group of sergeants and enlisted men to oust Céspedes. Ramón Grau St. Martin became

Cuba's new president. The leader of the military coup, Fulgencio Batista, was named as head of the nation's armed forces.

Working mostly behind the scenes, Batista controlled the Cuban government. After a quick succession of weak administrations, he ran for president in 1940 and won the election. That same year, the legislature ratified a new constitution, which gave workers the right to an eight-hour workday, guaranteed pensions, and social insurance. The constitution also guaranteed voting rights, freedom of association, and other civil rights. The Cuban economy boomed as sugar prices soared during World War II (1939–1945), helping to make Batista a popular president. He stepped down after Grau was elected president in 1944. Cuban voters elected Carlos Prío Socarras as president in 1948. Corruption, ineffectiveness, and violence, however, plagued his administration. Political opponents stepped up their opposition against Prío and hoped that success in the 1952 election would give them control of Cuba's government.

The Insurrection Begins

I n February 1952, a group of junior army officers approached Fulgencio Batista. The former president had remained a powerful figure in Cuban politics. He was serving as a senator in Cuba's legislature and was a candidate for the second time in the upcoming presidential election. The officers told Batista that they believed the country's political structure had completely crumbled. They asked him whether he would support a military coup to seize control of the government. With elections only four months away, Batista told them that a coup would throw the country into turmoil. As the officers passionately explained their reasons for overthrowing the Prío government, Batista realized that they would proceed with their plan with or without him. Having seen polls indicating that he was running a distant third, Batista knew that he had little chance of winning the June election. He decided to join the coup.

Before dawn on March 10, 1952, Batista arrived at Camp Columbia, accompanied by a group of officers. They arrested senior military officers and took control of the country's chief army base. Other officers seized key government buildings in Havana. Alerted to the coup, Prío rushed to the Mexican embassy, where he applied for political asylum. Batista released a public statement announcing the change in government. It asserted, "The military junta [has] acted to avoid the regime of blood and corruption which has destroyed institutions [and] created disorder and mockery in the State."[1]

THE 1954 ELECTION

Disappointed by years of political corruption and violence, many Cubans welcomed the new government. They had fond memories of Batista's presidency and hoped that he could bring out needed changes in the nation's political institutions. In his first speech, Batista promised to strengthen the nation's democratic foundations, boost its economic progress, and advance social justice for all Cubans. To assure the loyalty of the military and the police to him, Batista shrewdly increased their salaries. Even when he suspended parts of the nation's constitution, few Cubans voiced outrage.

Batista's power grab, however, did not please everyone. The new government postponed the 1952 presidential elections until 1954. The coup had taken the country's two major parties, the Partido Auténtico and the Partido Ortodoxo, by surprise. Each had hoped to gain control of the government in the election. Founded in 1934, when they elected Ramón Grau as president, the Auténticos claimed to stand for social justice and the protection of civil liberties. Grau's presidency, however, had failed to fulfill those promises. Once in power, the Auténticos had become mired in the same types of political corruption that had characterized earlier administrations. Unhappy with the direction that their party had taken, some members of the Auténticos had split off and started a new political party, the

In the decades before the Cuban Revolution, Cuba was a very popular tourist destination for Americans. Seen here, an American magazine advertisement from 1956 describes Cuba as the "Glittering Fun Capital of the Caribbean."

Ortodoxos. The Ortodoxo platform focused on honest government and social reforms. Its membership included a young lawyer named Fidel Castro, who was campaigning for a senate seat when the Batista coup ousted Prío.

THE BATISTA GOVERNMENT

When Batista seized control of the government in 1952, Cuba's economy was strong. The sugar boom that had started at the beginning of World War II continued into the early 1950s. North American firms built sugar mills, factories, and mining operations to extract cobalt, nickel, and other minerals. Tourism boomed. Attracted by Cuba's warm climate and hopping nightlife, tourists filled its beaches, as well as Havana's casinos, music clubs, and restaurants. All seemed well in Cuba. Beneath the surface, however, discontent began to build.

Although the country's overall prosperity had increased over the past decade, relatively few rich families held much of that wealth. Because of widespread government corruption and constant political turmoil, wealthy Cuban families invested a large percentage of their money abroad rather than in their own country. The country's economic growth since the 1940s had even rapidly increased the size of Cuba's middle class.

By the time Batista came to power, however, middle-class families had begun to struggle. The increasing price of imported goods, such as refrigerators and other desired modern conveniences, made it more difficult for them to maintain their standard of living. Conditions were far worse for the poor. Living conditions for rural factory workers and farm laborers had changed little. In rural areas, Cubans endured poor housing, few schools, and little access to health care. Outside of the big cities, Cuba appeared to be stuck in the previous century.

Despite its economic growth, Cuba remained dependent on the United States. It provided about 75 percent of Cuba's imports and bought about 66 percent of Cuba's exports. The sugar industry, the most important segment of the Cuban economy, relied heavily on the U.S. sugar quota. Government officials and wealthy families supported Cuba's close relationship with the United States. An increasing number of Cubans, however, began to believe that their country should seek greater economic and political independence from its powerful neighbor.

Although his hold on power seemed secure, Batista faced growing political opposition. Labor unions and workers voiced their unhappiness with the lack of job opportunities. Poor people complained about the decline in social services provided by the government. Middle-class Cubans fretted about inflation, which threatened their standard of living. Junior officers in the military complained about the lack of opportunities for advancement. Many Cubans voiced their outrage over continuing government corruption and political favoritism. Wealthy Cubans, top military officers, government officials, and foreign businessmen appeared to be Batista's only loyal supporters.

Confident that he had firm control of the government, Batista called for an election in 1954. Similar to many previous Cuban elections, however, the 1954 election turned into a farce. As election day approached, Ramón Grau, the Pardito Auténtico presidential candidate, learned that Batista's supporters were rigging the election. In protest, he dropped out of the race, citing widespread cheating. Despite running unopposed, Batista received only 40 percent of the vote. He moved into the Presidential Palace anyway.

The election was a turning point for many young Cubans who had become disillusioned with their country's political institutions. For decades, the electoral process had resulted mostly in corrupt governments that failed to uphold the rights guaranteed by the 1940 constitution and improve the social welfare of the country. Students and other young people began to believe that armed insurrection was the only way to overthrow the old political order and create a government that would provide justice for all Cubans.

Soon after the 1954 election, several groups, composed mostly of college students and young people, rose up to oppose the Batista regime. The Directorio Revolucionario Estudiantil (DRE), led by Antonio Echevarría, began a campaign of resistance. They burned buses, set off bombs in government buildings, and conducted other acts of sabotage against the Batista regime. Another armed revolutionary group, Segundo Frente Nacional del Escambray ("Second National Front of the Escambray"), led by Eloy Gutiérrez Menoyo, attacked the government from its base in the Escambray Mountains in central Cuba. A third group, the Movimiento 26 de Julio (M-26-7), was reorganizing to fight against Batista.

THE ORIGINS OF THE M-26-7

Fidel Castro, a frustrated Ortodoxo candidate, led the M-26-7. Soon after the 1952 coup, his group amassed weapons and ammunition on a farm outside of Santiago in eastern Cuba. They were training for an operation to overthrow the Batista government. Their plan was to attack the Moncada army barracks, a major military post in Santiago. Dressed as soldiers, the revolutionaries wanted to make the attack look like a military mutiny against Batista. This apparent uprising, they calculated, would trigger a conflict between different factions within the military and lead to Batista's downfall.

The poorly planned attack, which occurred on July 26, 1953, was a complete failure. Because the barracks stood at the top of a hill, the soldiers had the better combat position when Castro's revolutionaries launched their surprise attack. Unable to fight an uphill battle and greatly outnumbered, the revolutionaries fled in a disorganized retreat. The rebels killed only a few soldiers, but about 60 rebels were killed and others were soon captured. Soldiers immediately executed some rebels. Fidel and Raúl Castro fled into the nearby countryside but were quickly captured. In a stroke of good luck, they were transferred to a police station in Santiago. If they had been transported back to the military base, they likely would have been executed.

Outraged at the attack against his troops, Batista ordered the military to shoot 10 revolutionaries for each dead soldier. The military executed another 70 guerrillas. Many citizens condemned Batista for this harsh reaction. Two months later, the trial for the guerrillas began. Fidel Castro, who would be tried in a separate trial, defended more than 100 suspects. M-26-7 rebels were among the accused, but most were local people who had no connection to the attack. They were merely known to oppose the Batista government. The court found only 26 of the defendants guilty. Most received light sentences. As one of the leaders of the attack, Raúl Castro was sentenced to 13 years in prison.

On October 16, Fidel Castro appeared before the same court. Arguing in his own defense, Castro stood up and delivered an impassioned two-hour speech. He justified the attack by cataloging the crimes of the Batista government and provid-

AN M-26-7 REVOLUTIONARY REMEMBERS THE MONCADA BARRACKS ATTACK

Vilma Espín, Celia Sánchez Manduley, and Haydée Santamaría were among the women who played vital roles in the Cuban Revolution. Thirty-one years old at the time of the attack on the Moncada barracks, Santamaría later recalled the death of fellow revolutionaries, including her brother:

> Anything could have happened under the bullets, under the burst of machine guns, among the cries of pain of those who fell wounded, among the last moans of those who were dying. . . . I went to the Moncada with the people I most loved. . . . Cuba was at stake, the dignity of our offended people and their violated freedom, and the revolution that would turn people's destiny to their own hands. . . .

ing legal and moral arguments to support armed revolution against the regime. He also outlined his movement's plan to reform the government of Cuba. No one made a written record of the speech, but Castro later re-created it. He ended his speech with words that would become famous: "Sentence me. I don't mind. History will absolve me."[2]

Unimpressed by Castro's speech, the court sentenced him to 15 years in prison. Transferred to the Isla de Pinos prison, he joined his brother and other M-26-7 members. While in prison, Castro read books on history, philosophy, and economics. He had spent 19 months behind bars when Batista decided to release all political prisoners. On May 15, 1955, Castro returned to Havana. Despite the failure of his plan,

There are those moments during which nothing can shock you, either death, the bursts of machine gun fire, the smoke, the smell of burnt, bloodied and dirtied flesh . . . nor blood on one's hands. . . .

There is that moment at which everything can be beautiful and heroic. That moment at which life, however much it means and however important, challenges and conquers death.

The man approached. We felt another burst of gunfire. I ran to the window. Melba [a friend] ran behind me. I felt Melba's hands on my shoulders. I saw the man approach me and I hear a voice say: "They have killed your brother." I felt Melba's hands. I felt again the noise of the lead riddling my memory. I felt that I spoke without recognizing my own voice. "Was it Abel?" I looked at the man who lowered his eyes. "Is it Abel?" The man did not reply. Melba moved close to me. All of Melba was in those hands that accompanied me.*

* Betsy Maclean, ed. *Rebel Lives: Haydée Santamaría*. New York: Ocean Press, 2003, pp. 14-17.

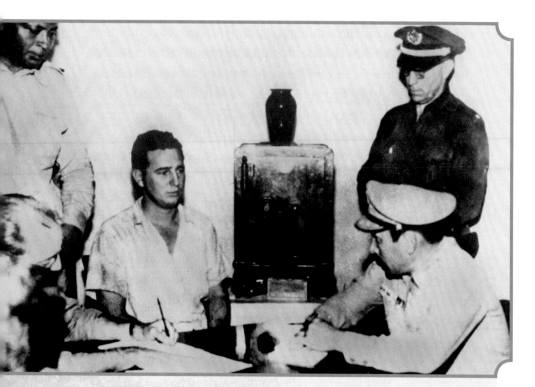

Here, Fidel Castro gives his deposition to officials of the Batista regime in July 1953. He had been arrested following the attack he led on the Moncada garrison house on July 26. Despite his impassioned self-defense in court, Castro was sentenced to 15 years in prison. He was released just 19 months later.

the attack on the Moncada barracks was a major turning point in the insurgency against Batista. Huber Matos Benítez, an M-26-7 commander, later observed, "No one quite knew what to do about Batista, and Fidel pointed the way—armed struggle."[3] The attack and the trials also thrust Castro to the forefront of the revolutionary movement.

After his release from prison, Castro spent several months in the capital. His former colleagues in the Ortodoxo Party shunned him. While Castro was in Havana, college students stepped up their protests against the regime's corruption. Other young people joined journalists and intellectuals in calling for a change in the government. In response to the protests, Batista ordered the police to arrest student protestors. As the protests grew, so did the violence directed at the protesters. Batista also began threatening newspapers that criticized his actions.

Castro once again concluded that the only solution to Cuba's political situation, as he wrote to a friend, was "armed insurrection."[4] He flew to Mexico in July 1955, following in the footsteps of past generations of Cuban political outcasts who found refuge abroad. There, he joined Raúl and began to organize a new guerrilla force. After training, they would return to Cuba and start a new rebellion against Batista.

GRANMA

In Mexico City, Castro circulated among other Cuban exiles, most of whom opposed the Batista regime. He soon became friends with Che Guevara. Through his extensive travels throughout Central and South America, this young doctor from Argentina believed that armed revolution was the only way to end poverty and social injustice in Latin America. Guevara described Fidel Castro in his journal as "a young man, intelligent, very sure of himself, and of extraordinary audacity."[5] The two men would later become compatriots in the insurgency against Batista.

Castro started raising cash to arm a rebel group to overthrow Batista. He visited the United States in November 1955 to attend fundraising events. Castro amassed enough money to rent a farm near Mexico City. He hired a retired Spanish military officer to train his men and bought a 60-foot (18-meter) boat. He would use the *Granma* to ferry his rebel army troops to Cuba once the men had been trained.

While Castro was preparing his men for battle, Batista came under attack from several directions. A series of troop uprisings unsettled the military, and by April 1956, several high-ranking officers began to conspire against the Batista regime. Politicians in the Auténtico, Ortodoxo, and

Communist parties began applying pressure on Batista in the national legislature. In November, students and faculty voted to shut down the University of Havana. Many students and young men in their late teens and early twenties would soon join revolutionary groups.

On November 25, 1956, the *Granma* departed Tuxpan, Mexico, with 82 revolutionaries aboard. Castro planned to land his men at Playa las Coloradas, located on the southwest tip of Oriente Province. Six decades earlier, Cuban independence martyr José Martí had come ashore near the same spot. Castro believed that he was completing Martí's work of bringing true independence to his country.

Castro coordinated the attack with a small group of M-26-7 revolutionaries based in Oriente Province. Led by Frank País, they would meet Castro's men at Playa las Coloradas and provide weapons, supplies, and transportation. They would also attack police headquarters and other government buildings in Santiago. The attacks would draw the army's attention to Santiago, enabling Castro's group to come ashore unnoticed and move into the Sierra Maestra Mountains. According to Castro's plan, the M-26-7 would launch an insurrection against Batista from the mountains, and it would spread throughout the country and overthrow the government.

Castro's plot quickly crumbled. When the *Granma* encountered rough seas, the 1,200-mile (1,930-km) voyage took two days longer than planned. By the time the ship arrived off the coast of Oriente on December 2, 1956, many of its passengers had become seasick. To make matters worse, the overloaded vessel ran aground on an offshore reef. The rebels had to wade ashore and then slog through a muddy swamp before reaching dry land.

Meanwhile, País had successfully carried out his part of the plan. One group of revolutionaries had launched an attack on Santiago on November 30. They held the city for much of the day but had to retreat when additional army units arrived.

Another group waited at Playa las Colarados with trucks to transport Castro's rebels. Hours passed, and the group eventually left the meeting point, thinking that the invasion had been canceled.

On high alert after the attacks on Santiago, the Cuban Navy became suspicious of the *Granma*. Soon after Castro's band arrived ashore, Cuban troops were tracking them. While Castro's rebels paused to rest in a sugarcane field near Alegría del Pío, Cuban soldiers fired on them. The men fled in different directions to escape the gunfire. Several rebels died, and Cuban forces captured and later executed more rebels. Two small groups of rebels, which included Castro and Guevara, managed to escape. It took them three days to find each other. Cuban troops then spotted them and attacked again. For more than a week, the rebels wandered around the swampy area, lost and hungry. They eventually met up with members of País's group.

Down to about a dozen men, Castro's rebel band retreated to the remote Sierra Maestra Mountains. There, they recovered and began to regroup and rebuild. With his plan of a quick overthrow of Batista crushed, Castro turned his attention to plotting a prolonged guerrilla war. He planned to use acts of sabotage to undermine the government. He also wanted to coordinate attacks with urban rebels in Santiago and Havana. He would later write to País, "We are in no hurry. We'll keep fighting as long as is necessary."[6]

Thereafter, the revolutionaries began their campaign of guerrilla warfare in earnest, attacking small army garrisons, exploding bombs, and destroying railroad tracks. After each attack, the rebels disappeared back into the mountains. As the on-and-off conflict between the rebels and the government continued, rumors surfaced that Castro was either dead or had left the country. In February 1957, the M-26-7 invited *New York Times* reporter Herbert L. Matthews to its headquarters. His story about Castro—along with a photo of the fatigues-clad rebel holding a rifle—appeared in the February 24, 1957, issue of the influential newspaper.

The article provided many Americans and people worldwide with their first glimpse of the charismatic rebel leader. Matthews wrote, "Fidel Castro, the rebel leader of Cuba's youth, is alive and fighting hard and successfully in the rugged, almost impenetrable fastnesses of the Sierra Maestra."[7] During the interview, Castro confidently told the reporter: "Cuba is in a state of war, but Batista is hiding it. A dictatorship must show that it is omnipotent or it will fail; we are showing that it is impotent . . . Above all, we are fighting for a democratic Cuba and an end to the dictatorship. . . . It is a battle against time and time is on our side."[8] In his article, Matthews added, "The personality of the man is overpowering. It was easy to see why his men adored him and also to see why he has caught the imagination of the youth of Cuba."[9]

M-26-7 attacks in Oriente Province increased to the point that the Batista government had to take action to quell the rebellion. Realizing that the people who lived along the lower slopes of the Sierra Maestra were assisting the M-26-7, the Cuban government borrowed a technique used decades earlier by the Spanish during their conflicts with Cuban independence fighters. The Cuban Army forced thousands of rural residents to leave their homes and farms. They moved them into government camps near Bayamo and Santiago. The government issued an order that any person found in the areas that it had cleared out would be assumed to be a rebel and shot on sight. A civilian vigilante group known as Los Tigres ("The Tigers") joined the government in its fight against the rebels. They intimidated, beat, and killed suspected rebel collaborators throughout the province.

Despite such harsh government tactics, the M-26-7 rebels continued to conduct hit-and-run attacks and retreat into the hills. They maintained contact with M-26-7 operatives in Santiago, Havana, and other cities. On several occasions,

Cuban revolutionary Frank País even managed to elude government troops to meet with Castro at his secret headquarters in the mountains. The M-26-7 also communicated with its supporters abroad. These supporters raised money and smuggled weapons and ammunition into Cuba. País's group then snuck the supplies to the rebels in the mountains.

Although initially isolated in the Sierra Maestra Mountains, the M-26-7 slowly transformed itself from a small, ragged band of rebels into a popular resistance movement. As the Batista government stepped up its concentration camp program, support for the M-26-7 increased, especially after conditions at the government camps, including poor sanitation and inadequate food and clean water, began to come to light.

Popular support for Batista plunged in other provinces as well. As the nation's economy worsened, unemployment began to rise. To many Cubans, the Batista government seemed out of touch. It cut public services and appeared unable to deal with a rise in robberies and other crimes. As the regime expanded its efforts to capture rebels and sympathizers, it ensnared many innocent people in its brutal interrogation program.

In May 1957, M-26-7 fighters overran army posts at La Plata and El Uvero. Each rebel victory—and each harsh measure adopted by the government—resulted in more recruits for the M-26-7. By the summer of 1957, many rural people had become Fidelistas, as M-26-7 rebels were often called. Oriente Province was a hotbed of revolution.

OTHER GROUPS IN THE INSURRECTION

Though growing in popularity, the M-26-7 was not alone in taking up arms against the Batista regime. One of the founders of the Ortodoxo Party, Rafael García Bácena, started the Movimiento Nacionalista Revolucionario (MNR). García, who had taught at Cuba's war college, had the support of many young military officers. When government officials became aware of the group, they arrested García and other MNR members early in the insurgency. Another group was the Organización Auténtica, the armed wing of the Auténtico Party, which was funded by former president Prío. It gained little support and remained a small operation. The Cuban Army or police eventually captured most of the Auténtico guerrillas. The Cuban Communist Party, the Partido Socialista Popular (PSP), also opposed the Batista regime. Led by Blas Roca, the PSP had attracted a modest percentage of votes in elections over the past two decades. With Batista's popularity plunging, the PSP began to make gains. Roca and other PSP leaders believed that it could gain more legislative seats—and perhaps even control of the government—through the electoral process. The PSP strongly opposed any group using armed insurrection.

The M-26-7's strongest rival, the DRE, stepped up its acts of sabotage and assassinations. DRE head Antonio Echevarría had met with Castro twice in Mexico. The two revolutionaries, however, had disagreed on many issues. Echevarría had refused to provide support for the *Granma* invasion. In March 1957, the DRE launched its most dramatic operation—a plan to assassinate Batista. Two groups of 150 DRE rebels attacked the Presidential Palace. At the same time, Echevarría seized control of Havana's main radio station. The DRE fighters successfully fought their way into the palace, but failed to locate Batista. By chance, he had left his office to visit his sick son in the palace's living quarters.

Broadcasting to the nation, Echevarría proclaimed that Batista was dead and called for a general strike to overthrow the remaining members of the Batista government. A technician, however, had switched off the microphone. The Cuban people never heard his call to arms. As Echevarría left the radio station, police gunned him down. Echevarría's death and the failed assassination attempt had three significant effects. It weakened the DRE. It motivated the Batista regime to increase its repressive measures of arrests, torture, and suspension of civil rights in order to identify revolutionaries and execute them. Most important, it left Castro's small, 100-person guerrilla army as the only serious insurgent force remaining in Cuba.

The M-26-7's capture of the army garrison at El Uvero signaled that Castro's group was still a threat. Guevara called the victory the M-26-7's "coming of age."[10] Castro's rebels began to expand their operations beyond their mountain stronghold. Using hit-and-run tactics, the rebels destroyed roads and railroad tracks, cut telephone and telegraph lines, and damaged bridges. In February 1958, Castro's rebels launched widespread attacks against sugar mills, tobacco factories, and oil refineries. They burned an astonishing 2 million tons (1.8 million metric tons) of sugar. The following month, Raúl Castro led 65 rebels into the Sierra Cristal Mountains on Oriente's northern coast. Juan Almeida Bosque led another group of rebels into a region north of Santiago. As the M-26-7 widened its areas of operation in Oriente, it began to make plans to expand the rebellion beyond Cuba's easternmost province. Castro and his rebels were eager to exert a greater impact on the nation.

The Rebels Win

On February 25, 1958, Fidel Castro made a public statement proposing a way to end the conflict. He would agree to a general election if government troops withdrew from Oriente Province. As the base of Castro's rebels, the province had become the focal point of the insurgency. Castro insisted that the Batista government would have to allow the Organization of American States (OAS) to supervise the election to ensure its legitimacy. If Batista rejected the offer, Castro vowed that the rebels would keep fighting. He asserted, "I do not believe in military rule. And there is a strong tradition in Cuba against military juntas. All Latin Americans are tired of government by colonels and generals. We do not want professional soldiers oppressing people."[1] Few Cubans were surprised when Batista rejected the offer.

THE GENERAL STRIKE

In late March 1958, the M-26-7 made plans for a widespread strike against the Batista regime. Its operatives in Havana and other cities did not always agree with the M-26-7 rebels fighting in the Sierra Maestras about which tactics to use. The urban rebels pushed for a national strike that would show Batista and the world that the Cuban people did not support his government. The previous year, a general strike protesting the killing of Frank País on a Santiago street had crippled Oriente Province. The strike had lasted for five days and had spread to other provinces. Castro had mixed feelings about the operation but eventually agreed to the strike. Havana-based M-26-7 rebel Faustino Pérez took charge of organizing the strike. Pérez had been a member of the *Granma* invasion force three years earlier.

The M-26-7 began lining up support for the general strike. Castro made a public statement, declaring that the Batista regime was near its end. He declared, "The entire nation is determined to be free or perish."[2] Pérez scheduled the strike for April 9, 1958. The exact date was kept secret to keep the government guessing. To set the stage for the strike, the M-26-7 and other rebel groups began setting off bombs in Havana in late March. Students across the country started boycotting their classes, forcing the government to close all public schools. Despite the promising buildup, the strike turned out to be a complete fiasco. Army and police officials had readied their men for any disturbances by rebels, workers, or students. Pérez had failed to get the needed support of the Communist Party or most labor unions, which could have persuaded workers to stay at home. On the day of the strike, M-26-7 and revolutionaries from other groups fired some shots in downtown Havana and briefly interrupted bus service and the telephone system. Most workers, however, went to their jobs. Most students, already not attending their classes because of the school closings, stayed home instead of joining planned protests.

BATISTA'S BIG PUSH

The failed general strike had a devastating effect on the M-26-7. It made Cubans question the rebel group's strength and effectiveness. Attacks against troops, acts of sabotage, and other rebel activities declined after the strike. Believing that it was once again safe to vacation in Cuba, some tourists began returning to the country by early May. The strike also hurt the M-26-7's reputation abroad. To assure exiled Cubans who were supporting and funding the rebels, as well as to preserve the neutrality of the U.S. government, Castro released a number of public statements. During an interview with a *Chicago Tribune* reporter, he tried to calm fears that the M-26-7 was a Communist organization. He told the reporter, "[n]ever has the [M-26-7] talked of Socialism or of nationalizing industries."[3] In other public statements, Castro spoke of working to promote better cooperation with other groups that opposed Batista, including rival revolutionary groups and nonviolent political parties.

The M-26-7's failed general strike also emboldened Batista. The revolution had nearly paralyzed the economy, slowing commerce and industry and reducing investments by Cubans and foreigners. It had scared off many tourists, leaving hotels, casinos, and restaurants almost empty. Batista believed that the strike revealed the weakness of the opposition groups and offered him a perfect time to counterattack. On May 24, 1958, the Cuban military launched an all-out offensive, known as Operación Verano ("Operation Summer"), against Castro's forces in the Sierra Maestra Mountains. Led by generals Eulogio Cantillo and Alberto del Rio Chaviano, more than 10,000 soldiers moved toward the mountains. Each army battalion had a tank unit and was provided air and sea support by the Cuban Air Force and Navy. The commanders planned to advance their troops into the mountains. The troops would sever Castro's supply lines and then steadily shrink the M-26-7's area of operation. Once the army had the area surrounded, it

Seen here, Cuban dictator Fulgencio Batista attends the Cuban Grand Prix car race in Havana. Following the failed general strike pushed by the M-26-7, Batista ordered the Cuban military to conduct an all-out offensive against the rebels in May 1958.

would use its greater numbers and better weaponry to overwhelm the rebel bands.

For the next two months, the military advanced to encircle the Sierra Maestras. The air force dropped bombs on Raúl Castro's rebel band, which was carrying out missions on the northern end of Oriente Province. Cuban troops slowly pressed forward, reducing the rebels' territory. The rebels fought back, ambushing army columns. Batista soon ordered about one-quarter of his troops to guard coffee and sugar plantations, fearing that the rebels would destroy them. By mid-June, the army had backed the rebels into a small area of about 4 square miles (10.4 sq km). The outlook for Castro's rebels, surrounded by the army on three sides, looked grim.

Despite the army's advance, the rebels managed to hold on. The army's large advantage in weapons and troops did not provide a complete picture of the combat situation. Army commanders had little actual warfare experience. Many had advanced due to family connections or a willingness to please

A COMPLEX LEGACY

Fulgencio Batista y Zaldívar (1901-1973) led two military coups that resulted in him ruling Cuba twice, from 1933 to 1944 and from 1952 to 1959. Born into a poor rural family, Batista worked at various jobs as a teenager and joined the army at age 20. In addition to his military duties, Batista attended night school and followed his own rigorous self-education program. He rose to the rank of sergeant.

In 1933, he led the military coup known as the Sergeants' Revolt that overthrew the unpopular government of Carlos Manuel de Céspedes. Batista was promoted to colonel and named to head the Cuban Army. In that position, he controlled the Cuban government. Backed by several political parties, Batista decisively won the 1940 presidential election. During Batista's four-year term, Cuba experienced economic growth and improvements in education and social services.

Voters elected Batista to the Cuban Senate in 1948. Four years later, he was a candidate for president when he joined a military coup that took only 77 minutes to oust Cuba's

Batista and his officials, rather than because of their military expertise or leadership abilities. Since few local residents cooperated with them, the army had little information about the M-26-7 rebels. It did not know how many rebels it was facing or how well armed the rebels were. Castro's fighters seemed to be everywhere and nowhere. The rebels successfully ambushed soldiers and quickly escaped into the jungle. Because of low troop morale and sympathy for the rebel cause, army soldiers had little motivation to fight. Some soldiers even switched sides. Many others remained in the army only

ineffective president, Carlos Prío. Batista served as interim president for two years until he won the 1954 presidential election, in which widespread voting fraud was uncovered.

Civil unrest broke out soon after the 1952 coup to protest the cancellation of the election. It intensified after Batista rigged the 1954 election. By 1955, several revolutionary groups had taken up arms to overthrow Batista's government. Batista responded to the armed rebellion by suspending constitutional rights and adopting brutal measures to punish rebels and their sympathizers. As a result of his policies, he soon lost the support of the Cuban people and the financial and military backing of the U.S. government as well. In the summer of 1958, Batista's war against the revolutionaries turned against him. As a small band of rebels led by Fidel Castro began to gain control of more territory, Batista's handpicked successor won a presidential election boycotted by most Cubans. His army's defeat at Santa Clara in December 1958 sealed Batista's fate. He fled the country on January 1, 1959, turning control over to a military commander. He flew to the Dominican Republic and later settled in Portugal. Batista died in Spain at the age of 72.

because they would be shot for desertion. Most of the soldiers had grown up in western Cuba, so even the dedicated ones did not know the area and were not accustomed to the terrain and climate in the mountains.

On June 29, 1958, one unit of the army's 11th Battalion was camped near Santo Domingo in the Oriente Province. Without begin detected, about 100 of Castro's rebels surrounded the troops on three sides. Rebel sharpshooters began firing their rifles, picking off soldiers. Although significantly outmanned and outarmed, the rebels killed or captured 64 soldiers and seized many weapons. This attack, one of the few major battles during the insurgency against Batista, demoralized army commanders and soldiers. It was a tremendous setback for the government.

Following their Santo Domingo victory, M-26-7 rebels launched attacks on other army positions. On July 11, 1958, Castro's forces surrounded the 18th Battalion near Jigüe. The clash resulted in the surrender of the entire 500-man battalion. Battalion commander José Quevedo Pérez and several other officers joined the rebels after the surrender. As the army began retreating from the mountains, mass desertions like this one became a problem. Problems soon grew worse for the government. Rebels managed to capture an army radio, along with the secret codes used by the army. Using the radio, the rebels issued orders that confused commanders and soldiers. They even successfully ordered an air strike on army troops. By the end of July, the entire Cuban Army had withdrawn from the Sierra Maestras. The failure of Operación Verano demoralized Batista's troops and boosted rebel morale.

During the two-month army offensive, fighting killed about 30 rebels and wounded about 50. The rebels took more than 400 soldiers as prisoners. Castro issued strict orders that they not be mistreated. The rebels provided wounded soldiers with medical treatment and then released most of their captives. Releasing prisoners had two benefits. The rebels did not have enough men to guard prisoners and had nowhere to house them. Releasing soldiers also provided good public relations. Castro repeatedly compared how each side treated prisoners. In one public statement, Castro trumpeted:

> Since January 1957 . . . some six hundred members of the armed forces . . . have passed into our hands . . . none have been killed . . . while torture and death have been the certain fate awaiting every rebel, every sympathizer, even every suspect who fell into enemy hands . . . killing has made nobody stronger. Killing has made *them* weak; refusing to kill has made *us* strong.[4]

While the battle raged in the Sierra Maestras, Raúl Castro led a group of M-26-7 rebels operating on the northern coast of Cuba. On June 26, Raúl's men moved down from the Sierra Cristal Mountains into Moa Bay, where they kidnapped 10 U.S. citizens and 2 Canadians working there. Raúl's unit also carried out other kidnappings, seizing sugar mill managers and even 27 U.S. sailors and Marines from Guantánamo, who had been returning to the naval base on a Cuban bus. Raúl then sent a letter to Earl Smith, the U.S. ambassador to Cuba, in which he promised to release all of the kidnapped persons if the United States stopped shipping military equipment to the Batista government. The earlier U.S. arms embargo had contained several loopholes, so some military hardware, particularly spare parts, still flowed into the country. Castro also demanded that the United States stop providing aviation fuel from its Guantánamo naval base to the Cuban Air Force. In early July, Raúl's men kidnapped six U.S. employees of the United Fruit Company.

The various kidnappings outraged the U.S. government. Secretary of State John Foster Dulles asserted that the United States could "not be blackmailed into helping the rebels."[5] He denied that the United States was supplying Batista with any military equipment or fuel. Although the M-26-7 kidnappings were risky because they angered the United States, they also put Batista in a tough spot. He could not assure U.S. officials that his government could return the kidnap victims unharmed. The inability to deal with the kidnappings showed Cubans and the U.S. government that Batista lacked full control of the country. The administration of President Dwight D. Eisenhower considered launching a military invasion to rescue the prisoners but decided that it would not ensure the safety of the prisoners. The rebels soon released the captives without gaining any concessions from the U.S. government. The operation lost the M-26-7 much of the goodwill that Fidel Castro had developed in the U.S. government, particularly in the State Department and the Department of Defense. It also lowered U.S. public opinion of Castro and the rebels.

On July 20, 1958, representatives of the various groups that opposed Batista met in Caracas, Venezuela. They signed the Pact of Caracas, an agreement to establish a unified effort to overthrow the dictator. The pact proposed that a temporary government rule briefly after Batista's ouster. It would restore constitutional and democratic institutions to Cuba. Castro was named as commander in chief of the armed forces of the unified insurgency.

As the rebels pushed back government forces, Castro moved his headquarters out of the mountains to a location near La Plata, a small coastal town west of Santiago. At that time, Castro's role began to change from military leader to political leader. In the regions that the M-26-7 held, he imposed a tax on sugar. Even the U.S.-owned mills paid the tax. His public statements began to focus on what steps should be taken to bring back democracy once Batista had been toppled.

From La Plata, Castro planned a three-point attack to end the rebellion. Castro and the main contingent of rebels would surround Santiago. Guevara would move his group of 150 rebels westward to the central province of Las Villas. They would cut off all telephone and telegraph communications between

A number of leading American politicians were outraged by the Cuban rebel kidnappings of U.S. citizens in Cuba. Among them was John Foster Dulles, who was serving as secretary of state under President Dwight D. Eisenhower. He vowed that the U.S. government would not be blackmailed into helping Castro's rebels.

Havana and eastern Cuba. Guevara's unit would also try to nudge out the other guerrilla groups operating in the region. At the same time, Camilo Cienfuegos and about 80 rebels would maneuver south of Havana and begin operations in the far western province of Pinar del Río.

As the conflict's momentum began to shift toward the insurgents, Batista ordered more extreme measures against rebels and suspected sympathizers. The military and police began beating and torturing captured rebels and suspects to gain information about rebel groups. Batista's crackdown began affecting an increasing number of middle-class Cubans, who heard stories of abuse and atrocities from friends and family members seized by Batista's secret police. Many became disgusted with the government and switched their allegiances to the rebels. By fall, rebel successes had had a major impact on Cuba's economy. Rebels controlled areas with many major sugar and coffee plantations. U.S. citizens working as managers in U.S. sugar mills and mines had left the country. Batista and the military still held Havana and the region around it, as well as such major cities as Santiago and Santa Clara. The government controlled other areas in the country, but rebel groups were gaining ground quickly. By mid-October 1958, Guevara and Cienfuegos, chief of the Camp Columbia army headquarters, had moved their troops into the Las Villas and Pinar del Río provinces.

Presidential elections were held on November 3. Because Cubans knew that the election would be rigged, many voters boycotted the vote. No one was surprised when Batista's candidate, Andrés Rivero Agüero, was elected. A longtime Batista ally, Rivero had served as prime minister before resigning to run as the Progressive Action Party's candidate. A *New York Times* reporter estimated that less than a third of voters showed up at the polls. In some regions, fewer than 10 percent of eligible voters cast a vote. Auténtico candidate Ramón Grau petitioned to have the election nullified. The House of Representatives, however, declared the election valid. Reliable evidence later showed that the military had printed and marked many of the ballots counted for Rivero.

When shown the fake ballots, Ambassador Earl Smith concluded that the United States should stop propping up the regime. Smith informed Batista that the U.S. government would not support the Rivero government. In a secret meeting, an unofficial representative of the U.S. government offered Batista safe haven. He could move his family to Florida, provided that he set up a provisional government that was acceptable to the Eisenhower administration. The United States would then ship arms to the Cuban military to prevent the M-26-7 from taking control of the country. Batista declined the offer.

While the election controversy continued to swirl, Batista's army was losing in the field. Officers began avoiding battles with the rebels. Some even ordered troops to stay in their barracks. Several officers surrendered to the rebels and joined Castro's cause. Batista ordered several other officers arrested for suspected sympathies for the rebels. By December, the government still held Santiago, but rebels controlled all of the smaller towns in Oriente Province. Castro's troops began to surround Santiago.

Batista made a last-ditch effort to rally his army. He ordered his commanders to send more than 1,000 soldiers to Santa Clara, the capital of the Santa Clara Province in central Cuba. Military intelligence had information that the rebels planned to blow up a key bridge there. The troops arrived in Santa Clara but could not prevent Guevara's unit from seizing the town. As M-26-7 rebels gained control of Santa Clara, General Carlos Tabernilla told Batista that the time had come to admit defeat: "The soldiers are tired and the officers do not want to fight. Nothing more can be done."[6] Tabernilla had already instructed General Cantillo to make preparations to negotiate surrender terms with Castro.

Just after the stroke of midnight on January 1, 1959, Batista informed his cabinet and closest colleagues that he was leaving the country. Batista later wrote, "After the disloyalties, surrenders, treacheries, and with only a scrap of the army left, there was only the prospect of a mountain of corpses."[7] He delivered his resignation to General Cantillo. Batista and his colleagues rushed to the airport at Camp Columbia. Shortly before 9 A.M., a Havana radio station announced "¡*Se fué Batista!*" ("Batista is gone!")

Castro
Consolidates
Power

The days following the fall of the Batista regime turned into a prolonged celebration for Cubans. The hated dictator had fled and the future looked bright. After their triumphant march to Havana, Fidel Castro and the M-26-7 had little time to celebrate. To bring down Batista, they had endured harsh conditions and hard times for more than five years. They had lost many friends. Now, they faced two significant challenges: building a new government and consolidating their political power. As Castro had told the crowd in Santiago on January 2, 1959, the Cuban Revolution had not ended. It had just begun.

Castro and the M-26-7 enjoyed widespread support from the Cuban public. Cubans of all ages, races, and economic classes supported them and viewed the rebels as the symbol of Cuba's successful struggle to achieve genuine independence and national unity. Castro and the M-26-7 leadership realized, how-ever, that they were not the only political forces in the country. They had to contend with other rebel groups—particularly the Directorio Revolucionario Estudiante, which had strong sup-port in Havana—as well as members of Cuba's traditional politi-cal parties: the Auténticos, the Ortodoxos, and the Communists.

THE FIRST CABINET

Fidel Castro and the M-26-7 leadership did not directly seize control of the government. Instead, they placed key support-ers—as well as potential rivals—in high government offices. As promised during the insurgency, widely respected moderate and former judge Manuel Urrutia was named president of the interim government. José Miró Cardona, a prominent lawyer, was named as prime minister. Although Miró had been one of his law school professors, Castro was wary of his former teacher's allegiance to the revolution. In fact, he had made sure that Miró had a role in the new government to prevent him from plotting against it. The first presidential cabinet included several members of the M-26-7. Most were lawyers and other urban professionals who had joined the unarmed political wing of the M-26-7. Only one member of Castro's rebel army served as a member of the first cabinet. The cabinet promised that elections would be held in 1961, once the interim government had stabilized the country.

Castro assumed the position of commander in chief of the army, now called the Rebel Armed Forces. Although not a part of the cabinet, he wielded tremendous power owing to his immense popular support. Appointed as defense minister, Raúl Castro began organizing a new army for the nation. Because of worries about his brother being assassinated by Batista support-ers or rival revolutionaries, Raúl was officially named as Fidel's successor. Fidel, however, dismissed the threat of assassination: "The destiny of peoples cannot depend on one man. . . . [A]ssas-sinating me would only fortify the Revolution."[1]

Following the successful overthrow of the Batista regime, Fidel Castro asked his former law school professor José Miró Cardona to serve as Cuba's prime minister. After just six weeks, he resigned as prime minister for being critical of Castro's policies and later sought refuge in the United States.

The composition of the first cabinet and its initial actions gave the impression that perhaps Castro's revolution would not be so revolutionary after all. The new government promised to restore civil rights guaranteed by the 1940 constitution and to enact moderate political and social reforms. Among his first official acts as president, Urrutia tried to close casinos, end the national lottery, and crack down on prostitution and other vices. The people who worked in these businesses, however, strongly opposed Urrutia's plan. Castro intervened and negotiated a deal in which Urrutia's plans would be postponed until the government could find jobs for affected workers.

The new cabinet created several new ministries to carry out political and social reforms. The Ministry of Housing and the Ministry of Social Welfare launched programs to reduce rents and to improve the well-being of Cuba's poorest citizens. Another new agency, the Ministry for the Recuperation of Misappropriated Goods, managed the task of dealing with the land and business assets abandoned by Batista and his friends when they had fled the country. Pressured by Castro, Urrutia and other high-ranking government officials announced that they were cutting their own government salaries to support the revolution.

The new government also set up price controls for telephone and electricity service, mandated price reductions for medicines, and introduced a minimum wage for sugarcane cutters. These programs received widespread support among Cuba's middle class and poor. They were highly unpopular, however, among wealthy Cubans and foreign businessmen affected by the new regulations.

THE TRIBUNALS

During the early days of the new government, members of the rebel army, led by Raúl Castro and Che Guevara, tracked down and arrested several hundred Cubans who had participated in the Batista regime. The government insisted that war tribu-

Following their consolidation of power, Cuban revolutionaries Che Guevara *(left)* and Fidel Castro *(right)* conducted military tribunals to try and convict people who had worked for the Batista regime. Around 150 ex-police officers and government officials were tried, found guilty, and executed in what many people viewed as show trials.

nals, or trials, be held to try those who had beaten, tortured, and killed for Batista. Camilo Cienfuegos, chief of the Camp Columbia army headquarters, asserted that "only those convicted of crimes of torture and killing" would be executed.[2]

Beginning in January 1959, more than 200 former policemen, government officials, and Batista supporters faced trial in Havana's main sports stadium. Cuban television stations provided live broadcasts of the trials. Large, seething crowds filled the stands shouting for justice. Cubans traumatized by the violent repression during Batista's reign supported the tribunals. They wanted justice—and vengeance—for themselves and other Cubans. About 150 defendants were found guilty and executed. The apparent score-settling and executions shocked some wealthy Cubans and intellectuals, who quietly began to question the fitness of Castro and government officials to lead the country. Newspapers in the United States and Europe portrayed the tribunals as show trials, in which the verdicts and punishments had already been decided. For many Cubans and foreign observers, the executions tarnished the revolution.

CASTRO TAKES CONTROL

Although Castro appeared to be taking a backseat in the new government, he soon exerted greater and more overt control. On February 7, 1959, the cabinet approved a new law that gave the power to make laws to the cabinet rather than to the legislature. Although the law violated the 1940 constitution, the cabinet argued that the measure was needed to move the country through the early stage of the revolution. Grasping that he now had no actual authority, Prime Minister Míró resigned one week later. He suggested that Castro take over the position because he held the real power anyway. Instead, Castro recommended Interior Minister Luis Orlando Rodríquez. Orlando also declined, saying that Castro should be prime minister.

In discussions with President Urrutia, Castro agreed to take the post if he was given broad powers to run the government. Urrutia realized that he was being squeezed out. He tried to resign, but members of the cabinet talked him out of it, telling him his service was needed for the revolution. Urrutia remained but became just a figurehead with no real influence in the government. He stopped attending cabinet meetings, and executive power essentially rested in Castro's hands.

In the early days of the revolutionary government, Castro spoke of holding elections by 1961. Once installed as prime minister, however, he declared that elections would not be necessary for the foreseeable future because he and the cabinet were ruling by the will of the people: "It is in the public interest that elections are delayed till political parties are fully developed and their programs fully defined."[3]

CASTRO VISITS THE UNITED STATES

In April 1959, Fidel Castro visited the United States to give a speech at a meeting of the American Society of Newspaper Editors. In Washington, D.C., he met with representatives of the Eisenhower administration and members of Congress. President Eisenhower had made sure that he was out of town during Castro's visit, but Vice President Richard Nixon had a meeting with the Cuban leader. In a memo to Eisenhower, Nixon reported, "Whatever we may think of him, he is going to be a great factor in the development of Cuba and very possibly in Latin American affairs generally."[4]

Castro's speech to the newspaper editors impressed the crowd. He appeared on the TV news program *Meet the Press*. When a reporter asked Castro about his ties to Communist elements, the Cuban leader replied, "Democracy is my ideal. . . . I am not a Communist. . . . There is no doubt for me between democracy and Communism."[5]

In New York City, a crowd numbering in the thousands gave him an enthusiastic welcome. Holding signs that read "¡*Viva la Revolucion Cubana!*" and "¡*Viva Fidel!*" ("Long live the Cuban Revolution!" and "Long live Fidel!"), the crowd even chanted, "Fi-del! Fi-del!" He held a press conference and appeared at a question-and-answer session at Columbia University. He also met with the publisher of the *New York Times*. Castro spoke of creating an economically and politically sound Cuba. At his last stop, a meeting of female lawyers, he told the gathering, "I simply was a lawyer who took arms for defending the law."[6]

THE AGRARIAN REFORM LAW

During the fight against Batista, the M-26-7 had promised to change Cuba's property laws, which had long favored wealthy plantation owners. On May 17, 1959, Castro announced the creation of a far-reaching land reform law. He said that it rep-

CASTRO ANNOUNCES THE NEW LAND REFORM LAW

On May 17, 1959, Fidel Castro announced the new Agrarian Reform Law in front of an audience of poor farmers at his former headquarters in the Sierra Maestra:

We are aware that this law will affect some private inter-ests; we are aware that it will find strong opposition, as [with] all revolutionary measures. . . . However, we must declare . . . that we make laws only for the benefit of the nation, even if these laws must sometimes damage certain interests. . . . What we have done, what we are, what we represent, and what we do are mainly conse-quences of the past. In fact, anybody in Cuba who thinks about what this country has been up to now, about the destiny which would have been Cuba's destiny if changes were not introduced, . . . she will have to admit that these measures are absolutely necessary. It was not fair that our country continue to go toward misery, toward chaos. . . . [T]he mistakes of the past generations are not ours. You do not understand this until you go to the country, . . . until you see shoeless, hungry, sick children who cannot read nor write. In spite of all this, you are surprised to see how much kindness remains in the hearts of our peasants. When you notice those things, you feel the absolute conviction of the justice of the measures

resented a "new era in our economic life, and that a wonderful future awaits our country, if we dedicate ourselves to work with all our might."[7] The act would forbid large estates. Landowners could keep 1,000 acres (404 hectares) of their property but had to surrender the rest. The government would divide the

we are taking, which are necessary and of benefit for the country. . . . The Agrarian Law damages an insignificant section of the people, but even these persons are not entirely sacrificed, as they will keep a considerable amount of land; their standard of living will not be seriously affected, and at the same time thousands of poor families will be benefited. We can very conservatively estimate that two hundred thousand families will receive these benefits . . . [W]hen the Agrarian Law is entirely applied, two million Cubans will have their income increased, and they will become buyers in the domestic market, which will be the basis of our industrial development. Through this, we expect to solve the economic problems of Cuba. On the other hand, the owners of the lands we intend to distribute shall not be robbed; they will be compensated. They will be paid in government bonds. . . . Great landowners must understand that their duty is to adapt themselves to the new circumstances. . . . They will have to produce technically, economically, trying to obtain all which is possible to obtain from the land. . . . It is criminal that there be uncultivated land in a country where people are hungry. . . . [N]o real patriot can fail to understand that this measure will be of benefit to the Nation. . . . We wish that all Cubans accept it as a fair measure which will offer extraordinary benefits to our Country.*

* Fidel Castro, "On the Promulgation of the Agrarian Law," May 17, 1959. http://lanic.utexas.edu/project/castro/db/1959/19590517.html.

confiscated land into small plots of 67 acres (27 hectares) and give them to poor Cubans. Before the Cuban Revolution, government sugar quotas led to landowners keeping some of their acreage unplanted. The new law would increase the country's agricultural productivity by giving this idle land to poor farmers, who would plant sugar and other crops.

To organize reforms under the new land act, the cabinet created the Instituto Nacional de Reforma Agraria ("National Institute for Agrarian Reform"), or INRA. Castro was named as the head of the agency. INRA soon became the central cog in the Cuban government. Its Department of Industry, headed by Che Guevara, took over the businesses abandoned by Batista supporters who had fled the country. INRA even had a 10,000-man military unit, commanded by Raúl Castro. At the height of its power, INRA oversaw the country's land reform, housing, health, education, transportation, and defense.

U.S. REACTION TO AGRARIAN ACT

The Eisenhower administration initially embraced the new Cuban government, recognizing it within a week of Batista's exit. The appointments of moderates Urrutia and Míro as president and prime minister had reassured the U.S. government—so much so that during Castro's visit to Washington in April 1959, representatives of the administration told him that the United States would provide economic assistance to Cuba.

Castro's announcement of the Agrarian Law, however, raised U.S. worries because it mandated that only Cubans could own land in Cuba. Most foreign landowners in Cuba were American citizens and companies. Despite Castro's promise that landowners would be compensated for seized land, the law solidified the belief among U.S. government officials that Castro was a Communist. In a communiqué sent to the Cuban government three weeks after the announcement of the Agrarian Reform Law, the Eisenhower administration voiced its concern over the legislation. It demanded fair compensation for American landowners and predicted that the land reforms would lower foreign investment and harm Cuba's economy.

Cuba's land reforms marked the turning point in the country's relationship with the United States. In June 1959, the National Security Council (NSC), which advises presidents on security and foreign policy issues, concluded that Castro needed to be removed from office. The objective of the U.S. government was now "to accelerate the development of an opposition in Cuba, which would bring about . . . a new government favorable to U.S. interests."[8] The Central Intelligence Agency (CIA) drafted a plan to depose Castro and presented it to President Eisenhower in October. The plan called for the support of Cuban opponents of Castro's government while making it appear that Castro's government toppled because of its own errors.

Although officials in the CIA and other government agencies talked a lot about Castro turning into a Communist, the U.S. decision to overthrow him may have been based more on economics than politics. In January 1959, at about the time the Batista regime fell, U.S. investment in Cuba exceeded $1 billion. Much of this money was invested in the sugar and nickel-mining industries. The revolution's land reforms threatened the major investments of many U.S. companies—something of which the Eisenhower administration was keenly aware.

During this period, the Cuban government had yet to develop any diplomatic relationship with the Soviet Union, the most powerful Communist nation in the world and America's Cold War rival. The Soviets had traditionally ignored Cuba, viewing it as part of the U.S. sphere of influence. Moreover, Castro himself had repeatedly disavowed any ties to Communism and insisted that the reforms being introduced were modest and aimed at correcting misguided government policies and improving the well-being of all Cubans. Yet, he also knew that Cuba's economic fate was closely tied to that of the United States. U.S.-owned companies employed nearly

150,000 Cubans. Nearly 60 percent of Cuban exports went to the United States, including more than half of its annual sugar output, and more than three-quarters of Cuba's imports came from the United States. Angering U.S. businessmen and the U.S. government was a risky proposition for Castro's government. Having taken up arms against a well-armed government, however, Cuba's revolutionaries were accustomed to taking risks for their cause.

DOMESTIC OPPOSITION GROWS

As the U.S. government's position on Cuba was shifting, domestic opposition to revolution also grew. Conflicts within the government were the first signs of trouble. They reflected a growing opposition—particularly from the country's wealthy and politically active class—to the direction that the revolution was taking. Pedro Díaz Lanz, the head of the Cuban Air Force, was the first official to protest publicly against the revolution. He complained about the government's requirement of political classes for soldiers. Díaz believed that the classes were meant to indoctrinate soldiers with radical ideas. Fearing for his safety after speaking out, Díaz fled Cuba in a small boat in June 1959. He was soon testifying before the U.S. Congress, claiming that Castro was a Communist. One month later, Castro forced the resignation of President Urrutia, who had voiced his opposition in published interviews to several new government programs. Noted lawyer Osvaldo Dorticós was named president. Before long, Castro was replacing any cabinet member who did not show full support for the revolution. By the end of 1959, all moderates would be ousted from the government.

In October, Huber Matos Benítez, a prominent rebel commander who had accompanied Castro on his triumphant march to Havana, resigned from the military. He had publicly claimed that Communists were infiltrating the new government. Government officials countered that he was cooperating with the CIA and supporting counterrevolutionary forces.

Matos was later convicted of treason and spent 20 years in prison. Troubled about the direction that the revolution was taking, other military officers resigned. Then, on October 28, 1959, a small airplane carrying Camilo Cienfuegos disappeared over the Atlantic. The country mourned the death of the popular M-26-7 commander. Rumors arose that either Fidel or Raúl had ordered him killed. Because Cienfuegos had never shown any disloyalty to Castro or the revolution, most historians have dismissed the speculation.

In August, counterrevolutionaries attacked Castro's house in a Havana suburb, spraying the residence with gunfire. At the same time, gunmen in Havana fired on a U.S.-owned electric company and a military armory. In a chilling echo of the Batista era, Castro ordered the arrest of Cubans who had voiced opposition to his government. Two hundred soldiers at an army base were arrested, along with hundreds of suspected counterrevolutionaries. Around the same time, rumors circulated across the island that former Batista officials were amassing soldiers and weapons in the Dominican Republic. The apparent threat of an invasion from the nearby island forced Castro to send troops to protect Cuba's eastern coastline.

By the end of its first year, the Cuban Revolution seemed under attack. Cubans wondered whether, like most of the nation's governments since independence, Castro's government would not rule the country for very long.

Defending
the Revolution

As the Cuban Revolution entered its second year, control over the island nation appeared to be slipping through the revolutionaries' fingers. In a remarkable twist of fate, Castro and his former revolutionaries were now defending their political power against domestic opposition, just as the Batista regime had done against them. Moreover, Cuban exiles were plotting to overthrow Castro's regime while Cuba's relationship with the United States was crumbling. To protect itself from its enemies and to carry out the revolution's agenda of political reform and social justice, the government would seek support from a nation that would lead to Cuba's becoming caught up in an international political and military crisis.

A NEW ALLY

In January 1960, the U.S. Congress debated a bill that would give the president the power to lower or end Cuban sugar quotas. The quota had helped support Cuba's sugar-based economy for decades. Since 1934, the United States had agreed to buy a certain amount of sugar from Cuba each year at a higher-than-market price. In 1959, the United States bought more than 3 million tons (2.7 million metric tons) of sugar from Cuba. Yet the quota also posed a problem for the Cuban government, since the U.S. government often used it to pressure Cuban leaders to pursue domestic policies desired by the United States.

The threat posed by the bill enraged Castro. He warned that his government would seize U.S. properties in Cuba if the United States lowered its sugar quota. Musing publicly about being free of the quota, Castro started a catchphrase that was repeated throughout Cuba: *Sin cuota, pero sin amo* ("Without a quota, without a master").[1]

As its relationship with the United States became increasingly strained, the Cuban government began to develop ties with the Soviet Union. The two countries, which had never maintained formal diplomatic relations, began trade talks in February 1960. The Soviet Union agreed to supply Cuba with crude oil, grain, and financial credit in exchange for 5 million tons (4.5 million metric tons) of Cuba's sugar over the next five years. It was a daring step for Cuba. At the time, the United States and the Soviet Union were in the midst of the Cold War, a period of intense ideological conflict and military standoff that dominated world politics. The Cuban government risked provoking the United States by conducting business with its greatest rival.

NATIONALIZATION

In April 1960, Soviet tankers arrived in Havana, carrying 300,000 tons (272,000 metric tons) of oil. The Cuban government asked the island's three oil refineries to process the crude oil. Three U.S. oil companies—Shell, Standard Oil, and Texaco—owned the refineries. Pressured by the Eisenhower administration, the companies refused to refine the oil. Outraged at the refusal, the Cuban government took action. During the month of June, it confiscated the oil companies' refineries, along with all of their other assets in Cuba. In response to the confiscations, President Eisenhower signed an executive order on July 6, 1960, reducing the remaining sugar quota for the year by 700,000 tons (635,000 metric tons). The quota reduction stunned Cuba. The Soviet Union, however, stepped in and offered to buy the allotment spurned by the United States. Another Communist country, China, also agreed to buy 500,000 tons (453,000 metric tons) a year for the next five years.

Then, on August 6, 1960, Castro announced that all major U.S.-owned properties in Cuba would be nationalized. That meant the Cuban government would take over ownership of the properties. U.S.-owned businesses in Cuba were vast, including electricity and telephone companies, factories, and sugar mills and plantations. In early September, Castro gave a speech in Havana that spelled out the new nationalization program. Cuba would take control of all U.S.-owned banks, railroads, port facilities, and hotels in the country. During the speech, he denounced the United States and discussed how the Cuban Revolution was part of the liberation struggles within Latin America. Castro also acknowledged Cuba's new commercial relationships with the Soviet Union and China but asserted that those countries had no control over the Cuban Revolution. The speech became known as the First Declaration of Havana.

On September 17, as Castro forewarned, the Cuban government seized all U.S.-owned banks in the country, including Chase Manhattan Bank and First National City Bank of New York. The following day, Fidel Castro arrived in New York City to address the United Nations General Assembly.

As Cuba's relationship with the United States cooled following the Cuban Revolution, another relationship warmed up: its association with the Soviet Union, America's Cold War rival. Here, Soviet leader Nikita Khrushchev embraces Fidel Castro at the United Nations in New York City in 1960.

In his address, he condemned the United States for its efforts to dominate Latin America and flaunted his new relationship with the Soviet Union.

When he returned to Cuba, Castro responded to assumed threats against his government from domestic opponents, Cuban exiles, and the United States. He announced the creation of neighborhood committees to watch for counterrevolutionaries. These neighborhood watches would eventually become part of the Ministry of the Interior and be known as the Committees for the Defense of the Revolution. In October, the Urban Reform Act went into effect, slashing rents by half. That same month, the government seized more U.S.-owned companies and nationalized nearly 400 companies owned by Cubans.

In response to the nationalizations of U.S.-owned companies, the Eisenhower administration announced economic sanctions against Cuba on October 19, 1960. An executive order banned the import of Cuban goods, including sugar, into the United States. The import ban was a powerful political weapon because Cuba's economy was so dependent on exports, particularly sugar, to the United States. The following day, the State Department recalled Philip Bonsal, the U.S. ambassador to Cuba.

By the time the U.S. economic sanctions began in January 1961, Cuba's revolutionary government owned about a third of the nation's farmland and controlled factories producing more than three-quarters of the national industrial output. The sudden nationalizations of U.S.-owned businesses, however, had created a problem. The U.S. citizens who had managed the factories and large-scale cattle ranches and sugar plantations had left the country. Few Cubans had enough training to manage such large-scale enterprises effectively.

Scrambling to make up for lost sugar sales to the United States, Minister of Industry Che Guevara traveled to the Soviet Union and other Communist countries in Eastern Europe to negotiate trade agreements. Although he had no formal training in economics or business, the famous revolutionary was an adept economic policy maker. He made plans to move Cuba away from its dependence on the sugar industry and to develop a new national economy based on industrialization. In Europe, he worked out deals with the Soviet Union and East Germany, Poland, Czechoslovakia, and other nations in the Eastern Bloc to buy 4 million tons (3.6 million metric tons) of sugar in 1961—a million more tons than the United States had been buying under its quota. The Soviets also agreed to export needed industrial equipment, such as factory machinery, to Cuba. Experts from the Soviet Union and other Eastern European countries would later provide guidance to Cuban officials struggling to manage their nation's economy.

THE YEAR OF EDUCATION

Facing the economic problems caused by the U.S. import ban did not prevent the revolutionary government from pursuing social programs to improve the country. The government designated 1961 as the Year of Education. About 40 percent of Cubans could not read. Its rural areas had few schools. As Castro had promised in his 1960 U.N. speech, the government launched a campaign to end illiteracy in the country. More than 100,000 teenaged students volunteered to take part in the campaign. They traveled the countryside, teaching poor adults and children who did not attend school how to read. By the end of the year, more than a million Cubans had become literate.

The literacy program became an important selling point for the Cuban Revolution. Teenagers who participated in the program became committed to the cause. It also gave poor rural citizens who benefitted from the program a good reason to support the government. After the literacy campaign ended, the government continued to support the education of adults, hoping that they would become more productive workers. It also hired more than 7,000 new teachers and built more than 3,000 schools, measures that allowed more than 300,000 students to attend school for the first time.

PLOTTING AGAINST CASTRO

When it became clear that the Cuban Revolution was not taking the path that the U.S. government and business interests had wanted, the Eisenhower administration authorized the CIA to draft a plan to overthrow Castro in mid-1959. On January 1960, a CIA proposal arrived on Eisenhower's desk that advocated sabotaging Cuban sugar refineries to cripple the

Cuban economy and in turn spur a popular revolt against Castro's government. Although Eisenhower thought that the plan did not go far enough, he authorized the CIA to proceed. The CIA provided funds and training to anti-Castro Cuban exiles. Using local counterrevolutionaries and sending small planes outfitted as bombers from airstrips in Florida, they destroyed sugar mills and other economic targets in Cuba. On March 4, 1960, in a haunting echo of the 1898 sinking of the *Maine*, a cargo ship delivering weapons from Belgium mysteriously exploded in Havana's harbor.

In January 1961, the administration of the newly elected president, John F. Kennedy, ended diplomatic relations between the United States and Cuba. That same month, Kennedy authorized the CIA to proceed with an invasion plan that it had drafted during the Eisenhower administration. Such a plan was not unprecedented. In 1954, the CIA had funded an invasion of Guatemala by exiled military officers, which succeeded in overthrowing the leftist government of Jacobo Arbenz, another Latin American government opposed to the United States. The CIA was convinced that a similar plan would work in Cuba. The plan focused on landing about 1,500 counterrevolutionaries on Cuba's southern coast. They would take control of the town of Trinidad and then move into the Escambray Mountains. There, they would join up with groups of anti-Castro rebels already based in the mountains. The landing force would call on all Cubans to rise up against Castro and declare themselves as Cuba's new government. The United States would air-drop weapons, food, and other supplies for the rebels.

While the CIA was secretly training the invasion force in Guatemala, the Cuban government took action against its opponents. In February 1961, the government captured and jailed 500 members of an underground resistance movement. The following month, government officials ordered the arrest of the leaders of other groups that had opposed the Cuban Revolution.

THE BAY OF PIGS

Despite the government crackdown, counterrevolutionaries picked up the pace of their attacks against Castro's government. They destroyed sugar mills and sabotaged public transportation. In April, bombs set off in Havana destroyed a major downtown department store. Then, two unidentified small airplanes dropped bombs on Cuban airfields, killing several soldiers and civilians. On April 15, Castro spoke at the funeral of a civilian killed in the attack. For the first time, he publicly announced the socialist nature of the Cuban Revolution. Speaking of the U.S. government, he declared, "This is what they cannot forgive, that we should here, under their very noses, have made a socialist revolution."[2] The following day, the CIA launched Operation Zapata, its planned attack against the Cuban government. To destroy the Cuban Air Force's ability to respond to the invasion, eight bombers piloted by Cuban exiles attacked airfields in Havana, Santiago, and other locations.

On April 17, 1961, CIA-trained Cuban exiles landed on two beaches located in the Bahía de Cochinos ("Bay of Pigs"). The invading forces met more resistance than they had expected because the Cuban government had begun organizing local militias throughout the country, arming farmers and laborers and providing them with basic military training. One of these local militias fired on the invaders as they came ashore. Alerted to the invasion, the Rebel Armed Forces used machine guns mounted on training aircrafts to attack the invaders and managed to disable several of the troop carriers. (The CIA's plan had called for a second bombing run to destroy any surviving Cuban military airplanes, but it was canceled for unknown reasons.)

The battle at Playa Larga became fierce. Although 160 Cuban defenders were killed, they prevailed over the invading force. Within two days, they had killed more than 100 invaders and captured 1,200 of the 1,500-man invading force. Cuban

The landing of Cuban exiles at the Bay of Pigs in Cuba in 1961 was a political disaster for the United States and an enormous victory for Castro's fledgling regime. Seen here, exiles are taken prisoner by Castro's forces after the failed invasion.

officials paraded the prisoners inside a Havana arena. Cuban journalists interviewed the leaders of the invasion on live TV. Most of the commanders had been army officers during the Batista regime, a few of whom later faced trial. Nine received sentences of 30 years in prison. Five were executed. The rest of the invaders were detained. The Cuban government would later return them to the United States in exchange for $53 million worth of food and medicine.

The botched invasion boosted the confidence of the Cuban government and solidified national support for the revolution. In fact, the Bay of Pigs dispelled the claims made by Cuban exiles that few Cubans supported Castro. Instead of setting off an uprising to remove him, as the CIA had planned, the invasion triggered a fierce defense of their country by everyday Cubans. It also strengthened Castro's control over the government and undermined the efforts of his opponents in the country and abroad.

The Bay of Pigs debacle deeply embarrassed the Kennedy administration and diminished the stature of the United States. It showed other countries, especially those in Latin America, that the United States could be successfully opposed. Despite this setback, the U.S. government continued to plot against Castro. In November, Kennedy signed a directive that asserted the United States would "help the people of Cuba overthrow the Communist regime from within Cuba and institute a new government with which the United States can live at peace."[3] The directive created a new program, Operation Mongoose. Its mission was to bring down the Castro regime. Operation Mongoose drafted a variety of plans, including assassination attempts. The Kennedy administration, however, never authorized any of the plans because each one would have required direct U.S. involvement.

TENSIONS RISE

In January 1962, the United States pressured other members of the Organization of American States to suspend Cuba's membership in the organization. A few weeks later, Castro gave a speech encouraging the citizens of all Latin American countries to oppose U.S. efforts to dominate the economic and political life of the Western Hemisphere. On February 7, 1962, President Kennedy announced a trade embargo on Cuba. Without food imports from the United States, the Cuban government began a program of food rationing. The following month, Kennedy expanded the embargo to ban the import of any goods that contained materials from Cuba.

The rift between Cuba and its longtime sponsor had grown too wide to ignore. The Bay of Pigs invasion and persistent rumors of CIA plots to assassinate him or overthrow his government convinced Castro that he needed to take action. He knew that his country did not have the resources to engage in a prolonged clash with the United States. His government needed protection against a direct U.S. attack or a U.S.-backed invasion. Losing the economic support that the United States had provided, Cuba needed new trading partners. Castro had one choice: to approach the Soviet Union. Since the end of World War II in 1945, the Soviet Union had expanded its domination over Eastern and Central Europe. It had tremendous influence over the Communist governments of Albania, Bulgaria, Czechoslovakia, East Germany, Hungary, Poland, Romania,

THE COLD WAR

The Cold War was a period of heightened tension between the United States and the Soviet Union that dominated world politics and public attention for nearly five decades. Major events during the Cold War included the Berlin Blockade (1948), the Korean War (1950-1953), the Vietnam War (1954-1975), and the construction (1961) and demolition (1989) of the Berlin Wall.

The Cold War began when the relationship between the United States and the Soviet Union deteriorated after World War II. The Soviet Union had joined with the United States, United Kingdom, and other countries to defeat Nazi Germany and its Axis powers allies. The political differences between Communism (in the Soviet Union and its allies) and democracy (in the United States and its allies), however, created a sharp division between the former allies. To guarantee its security, the Soviet Union took firm control of

and Yugoslavia. By the early 1960s, its powerful, nuclear-armed military rivaled the United States.

As the relationship between Cuba and the United States soured, the Soviet Union began to take an interest in the island nation. The Soviets wanted to expand their power and influence into Latin America and into developing countries around the world. Led by a charismatic revolutionary who looked favorably on socialism, Cuba appeared to be a good starting point. The Soviets also believed that Cuba, because of its location, would provide a long-term irritant to the United States. By early 1961, Soviet leaders had decided to invite Cuba to become their ally.

surrounding nations by installing Communist governments in these countries. The United States and its allies began to fear that Communism would threaten their national interests by spreading to other countries around the world.

For the next 40 years, the relationship between the Soviet Union and the United States swung between periods of open hostility and periods of lowered tensions. Because both sides had nuclear weapons, each was reluctant to engage in a direct conflict. A "hot" war between the two countries could destroy them. The battlegrounds of their "cold" war included lining up allies (either by persuasion or through political, economic, or military pressure), massive military buildups, espionage, propaganda campaigns, and clashing positions in the United Nations and other international organizations. The conflict also played out in wars between nations. In the Korean War, the Vietnam War, and the Soviet invasion of Afghanistan in 1979—as well as in other conflicts around the world—the United States and the Soviet Union inevitably backed opposing sides.

THE CUBAN MISSILE CRISIS

On May 29, 1962, a high-ranking Soviet military officer, Sergei Biryuzov, arrived in Havana. During a secret meeting, he informed Cuban officials that his government would agree to place nuclear weapons in Cuba to provide for the country's defense against the United States. Castro and his advisers discussed the proposal and considered its potential risks and rewards. Six weeks later, Raúl Castro traveled to the Soviet Union, where he told Soviet officials that the Cuban government would allow the Soviet Union to install the mis siles. Soviet troops would maintain complete control over the nuclear weapons and their launch sites. Raúl agreed that the pact would be signed and announced in November, when Soviet leader Nikita Khrushchev was scheduled for an official visit to Cuba.

The Soviets planned to set up 40 launch pads. Each pad would have two missiles, one of which would be armed with a nuclear warhead. To provide support for the missile sites, the Soviets would also send 42,000 soldiers, 42 MIG jet fighters, 42 bombers, 12 missile-carrying submarines, and conventional cruise and surface-to-air missiles to defend the launch sites.

The Castro brothers worried that the Soviets would not be able to transport all of this equipment and personnel across the Atlantic Ocean without the United States detecting it. They pushed the Soviets to publicize the military pact, believing the announcement itself would deter the United States. Convinced that U.S. officials would have no effective response once the missiles sites were armed, the Soviets refused. The first Soviet troops began arriving in Cuba in August. To avoid detection, they arrived at different harbors at different times and traveled at night. The Cubans were right to be worried. U.S. intelligence noticed the increase in Soviet ships arriving in Cuban ports. On September 7, 1962, Kennedy asked Congress for approval to call up 150,000 military reservists. Two weeks later, Congress adopted a resolution that enabled the presi-

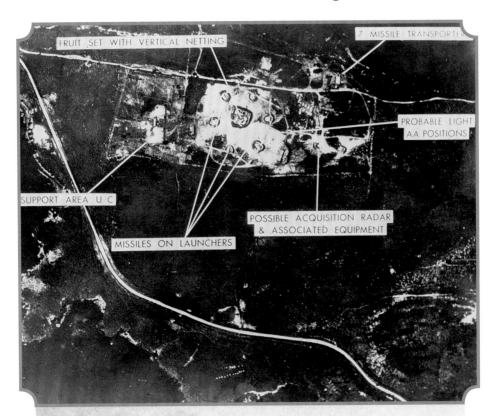

FRUIT SET WITH VERTICAL NETTING

7 MISSILE TRANSPORTE

PROBABLE LIGHT
AA POSITIONS

SUPPORT AREA U C

POSSIBLE ACQUISITION RADAR
& ASSOCIATED EQUIPMENT

MISSILES ON LAUNCHERS

This is an aerial photograph of one of the medium-range nuclear missile bases taken above Cuba in October 1962. The installation of Soviet nuclear missiles just 90 miles (144 kilometers) from the United States nearly led to an all-out war between the United States and the Soviet Union.

dent to authorize military action against Cuba to protect U.S. national security.

The first nuclear warhead arrived in Cuba in early October 1962. On October 15, U.S. military analysts noticed a familiar sight in reconnaissance photographs. The previous day, a U.S. U-2 aircraft had flown a mission over Cuba. Photographs made by the high-altitude spy plane's crew showed missile launch sites being constructed in the San Cristobal region of Pinar del Río. The analysts' findings were quickly relayed to the White House. Kennedy and his advisers met to discuss the development. The president then instructed military leaders to draft options for military intervention. They made plans for air strikes against the launch sites and for an invasion of Cuba.

The Cuban military noticed a sudden increase in activity at the U.S. naval base at Guantánamo Bay. Worried that the United States was preparing to launch an attack, Castro placed the Cuban military on high alert and informed the Soviets, who ordered their troops to be prepared for combat. The Soviet leadership did not, however, authorize commanders in Cuba to use nuclear weapons.

On October 22, Kennedy made a national television address. He told the American public that the Soviet Union was installing missiles in Cuba "capable of striking Washington, D.C., the Panama Canal, Cape Canaveral, Mexico City, or any other city in the southeastern part of the United States, in Central America or in the Caribbean area."[4] Noting that the longer-range missiles could reach as far as Canada, the president called the missile sites "a deliberately provocative and unjustified change in the status quo which cannot be accepted by this country."[5]

Instead of responding to the threat with air strikes or an invasion of Cuba, Kennedy had selected a third option. He announced a naval blockade of Cuba: "All ships of any kind bound for Cuba from whatever nation or port will, if found to contain cargoes of offensive weapons, be turned back."[6] He then shifted the tone of the speech and spoke directly to the Cuban people:

> [We] watched with deep sorrow how your nationalist revolution was betrayed and how your fatherland fell under foreign domination. Now your leaders are no longer Cuban leaders inspired by Cuban ideals. They are puppets and agents of an international conspiracy which has turned Cuba against your friends and neighbors in the Americas—and turned it into the first Latin American country to become a target for

nuclear war, the first Latin American country to have these weapons on its soil.[7]

Kennedy also warned the Soviets: "It shall be the policy of this nation to regard any nuclear missile launched from Cuba against any nation in the Western Hemisphere as an attack on the United States, requiring a full retaliatory response upon the Soviet Union."[8]

The U.S. naval blockade began two days after Kennedy's speech. To avoid a confrontation, the Soviets ordered their ships to stay away from the blockade zone. On October 26, Premier Nikita Khrushchev sent a letter to Kennedy, in which he wrote that the Soviets had sent the missiles to Cuba to prevent another invasion of the country. Khrushchev wrote that he would remove the missiles if the U.S. government agreed not to invade Cuba. The following day, Kennedy accepted Khrushchev's offer but insisted that U.S. inspectors verify that the missiles had been withdrawn. In return, America agreed to withdraw its nuclear missiles from Turkey—a minor concession because the older-generation missiles located there were considered obsolete.

The agreement between the two superpowers embarrassed Castro. The Soviets had agreed to U.S. inspections in Cuba without consulting him. He was also angry at the Soviets for making a crucial error. They used the same design for the Cuban missile launch sites that they used for their own launch sites. U.S. intelligence analysts immediately recognized the sites because they had seen them many times in reconnaissance photographs of the Soviet Union. Castro later observed:

> If we had known what those missiles were like, and if the question of camouflage had been posed to use, it would have been easy to decide what to do . . . it would have been the easiest thing in the world to build all those installations under roofs . . . and they would never have been discovered.[9]

Responding to the agreement between the Soviets and the Americans, Castro issued a statement on October 28. He made a variety of demands, including that the United States end its embargo, stop violating Cuba's airspace, and abandon its naval base at Guantánamo. U.S. officials ignored him.

The Soviets promptly dismantled the missile sites and removed their troops and weapons from the island. At a press conference on November 20, Kennedy announced the official end of the crisis. He told reporters, "We will not, of course, abandon the political, economic and other efforts of this hemisphere to halt subversion from Cuba nor our purpose and hope that the Cuban people shall some day be truly free. But these policies are very different from any intent to launch a military invasion of the island."[10]

The U.S. government would follow the policy that Kennedy announced. It maintained its anti-Castro rhetoric and its efforts to keep Cuba isolated and continued encouraging anti-Castro Cuban exiles to harass the Cuban government. In December 1962, Kennedy appeared at a ceremony in Miami that welcomed the Bay of Pigs detainees back to the United States. Although the administration had ended Operation Mongoose, the U.S. government set up a new agency to plan attacks against Cuban ships, acts of sabotage, and occasional attacks on the Cuban coast.

The Revolution
Endures

After the Cuban Missile Crisis, Nikita Khrushchev invited Fidel Castro to Moscow. The Cuban leader arrived on April 28, 1963. Castro stayed in Moscow for a week, meeting with Soviet officials and attending ceremonial dinners. He then embarked on a grueling, month-long tour across the Soviet Union. Large, enthusiastic crowds met Castro wherever he went. The successful visit helped soothe the Cuban government's bitterness over how the Soviets had handled the Cuban Missile Crisis.

Castro returned home in June, a period in which tensions between Cuba and the United States remained high. In the fall of 1963, however, Castro and President Kennedy both made public statements offering hope that the two countries could coexist peacefully. Any immediate hope of working out differences, however, ended when Kennedy was assassinated on November 22, 1963.

In January 1964, Castro made a second visit to the Soviet Union. This time, his meetings with Soviet officials focused on economic issues. Khrushchev agreed that the Soviet Union would buy Cuban sugar at a generous price of six cents a pound until 1970. It would buy 2.1 tons (1.9 metric tons) in 1965 and increase its order to 5 million tons (4.5 metric tons) by 1967. This agreement tied Cuba's fate to sugar for the foreseeable future. Decreasing the Cuban economy's dependency on the sugar industry was among the reforms that Castro had announced in the early days of the Cuban Revolution. Now, the revolution would abandon the industrialization program initiated by Che Guevara. The focus of the Cuban economy would return to sugar production.

THE EXODUS

Throughout the Cuban Revolution, many Cubans decided to leave their homeland. The first wave of Cubans to flee consisted mostly of people with strong ties to the Batista government. The executions of government and military officials soon after Batista's departure provided a clear signal to Batista supporters that it was time to leave the country. A second wave of emigration began in 1960 when the government began nationalizing domestic companies. This wave mostly included wealthy and middle-class Cuban families whose businesses had been seized. Most settled in the United States, particularly in southern Florida. As many as 40,000 Cubans left the country during the first two years of the Cuban Revolution.

The next wave of departures began when Castro became more radical. Many Cubans did not approve of the country's movement toward socialism. During 1961 and 1962, a total of about 150,000 Cubans left the country. Children made up a significant portion of these exiles. A program known as Operation Pedro Pan began on December 26, 1960, which allowed parents desperate for their children to escape Cuba to send them to the United States. Over the next two years, Operation Pedro Pan airlifted more than 14,000 Cuban children to Florida. Assuming that Castro's regime would not last long, many parents remained in Cuba and expected their children to rejoin them soon. For many families, however, the separation became permanent.

Cubans wanting to flee the country faced many hurdles. They had to go through a complex bureaucratic process to receive approval from the Cuban government. To settle in the United States, they had to apply for a special immigrant visa. Complicating matters even more, all commercial flights to the United States had stopped during the Missile Crisis. As a result, after October 1962, the rate of Cuban emigration declined sharply. Over the next several years, many Cubans decided to make their escape by boat.

In September 1965, Castro announced that participation in the revolution was voluntary. He assured Cubans that the government would not prevent anyone from leaving. To make boat transportation more accessible, the government designated the harbor at Camarioca, located on Cuba's northern coast, as the country's legal departure point. Thousands of Cubans descended on Camarioca. Cuban exiles in Florida hired boats to pick up friends, relatives, and even strangers. The passage across the open waters of the Florida Straits was treacherous. Small boats carrying Cubans, many helmed by inexperienced captains, frequently capsized or sank. Many Cubans drowned trying to reach the United States.

Overwhelmed by so many refugees and seeking to end the deaths at sea, the U.S. government approached the Cuban government. In November 1965, Castro called a halt to the boatlift. Three thousand refugees had already departed from Camarioca. Two thousand more remained there awaiting transport. The U.S. and Cuban governments agreed to set up an airlift to transport Cubans whose immigration applications had been approved. Flights began in December. Ten flights a week departed from the Varadero Airport near Camarioca. The airlift would continue until 1971, carrying more than 260,000 Cuban refugees to the United States.

The revolution benefited from the departure of the first wave of exiles. Many of Castro's political opponents were among those who emigrated. Their departures also made it clear to Cubans that the country's old political and social order had come to an end. The later waves of emigration, however, harmed the revolution and Cuban society. The mass exodus drained Cuba of its middle class and many of its most productive workers. The country lost many doctors, lawyers, college professors, and business owners. In the first two years of the revolution alone, more than 50 percent of Cuba's doctors and teachers left the country.

Many Cuban immigrants started new lives for themselves in the United States, in Spain, and in countries throughout Latin America. Cuba had a long history of exiles living abroad, either for economic or political reasons. In fact, many exiles had funded Cuban independence movements. During the post-independence period, opposition party leaders had often left Cuba to plot the overthrow of the party in power. Similarly, much of the Cuban Revolution had been planned and funded from abroad. Cubans fleeing the Cuban Revolution built a flourishing Cuban-American community in Florida, which would soon become a hotbed of anti-Castro groups. Cuban exiles and Cuban Americans would work tirelessly for decades to bring down the Castro regime.

SPREADING THE REVOLUTION

While forming their own government, Cuban leaders began to export revolutionary ideas to other countries in Latin America, advocating the toppling of dictators of the Dominican Republic, Nicaragua, and other nations in the Caribbean and Central and South America. They would later expand these efforts to Africa. Guevara proclaimed, "We have shown that a small group of resolute men, supported by the people and not afraid to die if necessary, can take on a disciplined regular army and completely defeat it."[1]

The Cuban government started promoting guerrilla warfare in Latin America in 1962. The first hint of exporting revolution came during a February 1962 speech by Castro, known as the Second Declaration of Havana. In his address, Castro declared:

> What is it that is hidden behind the [American] hatred of the Cuban Revolution? . . . What explains it is fear. Not fear of the Cuban Revolution but fear of the Latin American revolution . . . fear that the plundered people of the continent will seize the arms from the oppressors and, like Cuba, declare themselves free people of America.[2]

Castro, Guevara, and the M-26-7 rebels had inspired many young people throughout Latin America, some of whom hoped to duplicate the Cuban Revolution in their own countries. Cuba would go on to provide military training, weapons, and money to rebel groups in various countries. In some instances, it even provided fighters. The Cuban government assisted groups seeking to depose U.S.-backed leaders in Nicaragua, Panama, Guatemala, Peru, and Venezuela.

In 1962, Guevara tried to spark a revolution in his home country of Argentina. Cuba provided training to a group of Argentine rebels, but by the time they returned to Argentina, a civilian government had replaced the unelected military regime. The rebels found little support for their cause. Guevara then turned his attention to Venezuela. Local Communist factions agreed to support an armed insurrection against the government of Rómulo Betancourt. Cuba helped land small guerrilla units on Venezuela's coast after providing them training and supplies, but the rebels failed to incite an uprising. Minor fighting continued in rural areas in Venezuela for several years, but it had no effect on changing the nation's government.

In 1965, Peru's military crushed several armed revolutionary groups supported by Cuba. Weak insurgencies supported by Cuba in Guatemala and Colombia also flickered out.

Despite its failures in exporting revolution to Latin America, Cuba involved itself in several revolutionary movements in Africa. Although European nations had long controlled much of Africa, 17 former European colonies in Africa gained their

DEATH OF A REVOLUTIONARY

After returning from Africa in 1965, Che Guevara began working with Bolivian Communist rebels who were trying to overthrow the government of René Barrientos. Cuba provided training for the rebels, and Guevara and a small group of Cuban fighters accompanied them back to Bolivia. Guevara and the Cubans began conducting guerrilla warfare in remote areas of the country, hoping to trigger an uprising. A rift soon developed in the Bolivian Communist Party, however. Because the party had won several races in the 1966 elections, party leaders decided to stop participating in the armed rebellion against the government. Despite this, some Communist factions, including the one that Guevara had joined, continued to fight.

Back in Cuba, members of the government began to question the wisdom of exporting revolution. The efforts had not been successful, and the Soviets had expressed their disapproval of Cuban rebels stirring up trouble in Latin America. At the time, Soviet officials were making efforts to improve their country's relationship with the United States. Soviet officials warned Castro that Soviet economic assistance would end if Cuba continued support-independence in 1960. As liberation movements erupted in other countries on the continent, Cuba began assisting revolutionaries in Angola, Guinea-Bissau, Mozambique, Southern Rhodesia (now Zimbabwe), and the Congo (now Democratic Republic of the Congo). Guevara decided that Cuba should focus its efforts on the Congo because "victory there would have repercussions throughout the continent."[3] In April 1965,

ing revolutions in countries friendly to the United States. In October 1967, the Bolivian Army began an offensive against the guerrillas. It wiped out one group and surrounded another group, which included Guevara and the Cuban fighters. Guevara was wounded and captured. The Bolivian Army executed the 39-year-old revolutionary on October 9, 1967.

On October 18, half-a-million Cubans assembled in Havana's Plaza de la Revolución to mourn Guevara's death. Castro spoke to the crowd, paying tribute to his friend:

> They who sing victory over his death are mistaken. They are mistaken who believe that his death is the defeat of his ideas, the defeat of his tactics, the defeat of his guerrilla concepts. . . . If we wish to express what we want our children to be, we should say from our hearts as ardent revolutionaries: "We want them to be like Che!"*

Guevara's death and writings inspired revolutionaries worldwide, and an iconic photograph of Che taken in 1960 became one of the most printed photographs ever, appearing on T-shirts and posters more than four decades after his death.

* Fidel Castro, *Che: A Memoir*, New York: Ocean, 2005, p. 97.

he led a group of 14 black Cuban guerrillas into the Congo from Tanzania. Soon, 100 Cuban guerrilla fighters were in Tanzania. By November, however, the Cubans left when the leaders of the rebellion decided to stop fighting.

After the failure in the Congo, Cuba would avoid African causes for a decade. In 1975, however, Castro would send Cuban troops to Angola to help Agostinho Neto, a former rebel who had become the country's first president. Angola had always been a major concern in Cuba because many black Cubans traced their heritage to the African nation. Neto faced almost certain defeat at the hands of a South African invasion force when Cuban troops arrived to assist the Angolans. South African forces eventually retreated. In this instance, Cuban assistance had been effective. Some Cubans stayed behind to help the Angolan Army fight against other groups seeking to oust Neto.

¡LOS DIEZ MILLONES VAN!

By the late 1960s, sugar production had once again become the driving force of the Cuban economy. The Cuban government believed that expanding sugar production was the best way for it to raise cash to pay for imported goods. Because the sugar agreements with the Soviet Union had guaranteed a market for Cuban sugar, the Cuban government, with Soviet assistance, began to modernize its sugar industry. It built new sugar mills and introduced new technologies to harvest sugarcane. It also upgraded sugar warehouses, railways, and port facilities.

Despite the modernization efforts, sugar production rose slowly. In 1968 and 1969, Cuba produced only 3.7 million tons (3.36 metric tons) of sugar each year. Convinced that the country could do better, Castro announced a bold production target of 10 million tons (9.07 metric tons) for 1970. The 10-million ton harvest, he asserted, would solve Cuba's economic problems. The harvest, and its slogan, "¡Los diez millones van!" ("We will bring in the 10 million!"), inspired Cubans. Between November 1969 and July 1970, Cubans from all walks of life—from government officials and soldiers to college students and schoolchildren—pitched in. The efforts of nearly the entire population were directed toward sugar production. The government even abolished holidays during the harvest season.

It soon became clear to officials that the target could not be reached. Castro fired the head of the sugar ministry when the minister merely suggested that the quota might not be met. In the end, Cubans harvested 8.5 million tons (7.7 metric tons) of sugar. Although it was an amazing feat, all the hype made the accomplishment seem like a defeat. Because so many workers and resources had been diverted to sugar production, the excessive focus on the sugar target had harmed other areas of the nation's economy. In 1971, Cuba produced 5.9 million tons (5.35 metric tons) of sugar, and its annual production stayed about the same over the several next decades.

In the eyes of many Cubans, the failure had been Castro's fault because it was his personal project. The failure also focused public attention on Cuba's stagnant economy and revealed a disturbing problem in the government: The target had been announced despite limited discussion. No government officials had voiced their concerns because they did not want to speak up against Castro.

A CLOSER PARTNERSHIP

In 1968, Cuba entered into a closer alliance with the Soviet Union. Before then, the Cuban government had accepted military and economic assistance from the Soviets. Castro concluded that he needed more from the Soviets than just assistance; he needed economic advice, technology, and financial support. The Soviets had successfully managed their revolution for more than 50 years. Castro convinced himself that the Cuban Revolution could succeed if he adopted the Soviet model, including a one-party system of government. To achieve this goal, he would have to strengthen Cuba's Communist Party.

Castro had never been a traditional Communist. As previously mentioned, his M-26-7 and the Cuban Communist Party had been rivals during the insurgency against Batista. Although Castro had declared that the revolution was socialist in nature, nothing in Cuba resembled the highly controlled governments and economies of the Soviet and Eastern Bloc nations. That was about to change.

In March 1968, Cuban officials began restructuring the nation's government, economy, and society. They seized control of all remaining private businesses, including small stores, groceries, and the shops of barbers, carpenters, and plumbers, and clamped down on open political debate. Castro publicly supported the Soviet Union when it sent tanks into Czechoslovakia in 1968 to oust that country's elected government officials, who had promised reforms. Castro's announcement shocked many Cubans and lost Castro the support of many European liberals and socialists who had continued to defend the revolution. For the next 20 years, Cuba would shape itself into the Soviet Union's mold.

In 1972, Castro traveled throughout Eastern Europe for two months. In December, he signed a 15-year economic agreement with Soviet leader Leonid Brezhnev. Under the agreement, the Soviet Union would increase the price it paid for sugar and would substantially boost its financial assistance to Cuba. Cuba also joined the Council for Mutual Economic Assistance (Comecon), the economic union of Communist countries that controlled the trading relationships between the Soviet Union and its allies.

When Soviet advisers arrived in Cuba to provide guidance, Castro turned the planning and management of the national economy over to them. In 1976, Cuba announced its first five-year economic plan. (Five-year plans had long been a common feature of economic planning in Communist countries.) For the next decade, Cuba achieved an annual rate of economic growth of 4 percent. This accomplishment far outpaced the

Here, Fidel Castro speaks to the National Assembly in 1976, the year the Council of Ministers transferred its power to this new legislative body. The entire effort was more or less a show—the Communist Party, led by Castro, still had the final word in all affairs of state.

average 1.2 percent annual growth in Latin America during the same period.

Following the recommendations of Soviet advisers, Castro reorganized the Cuban government. He revamped the Council of Ministers, now numbering eight members. He merged the offices of prime minister and president and appointed himself to the office. The government approved a new constitution that provided for increased popular participation in government. In December 1976, the Council of Ministers transferred its powers to the National Assembly. Castro announced, "At this moment, the Revolutionary Government . . . places in the hands of this assembly the constituent and legislative functions which it has exercised for almost 18 years."[4] Despite its name, the National Assembly wielded little real power; it instead simply carried out the wishes of the Communist Party.

By the mid-1970s, the revolutionary government had transformed Cuba into a Communist nation. With the help of Soviet funding, it improved education and health standards, raised living standards, and increased the availability of consumer goods. At the same time, the revolutionary government had quashed internal dissent. Adopting some of the same repressive methods of the Batista regime, Castro's government had silenced or imprisoned Cubans who criticized it.

THE MARIEL BOATLIFT

In April 1980, the Cuban Revolution faced a major crisis. A small group of Cubans crashed a truck through the gates of the Peruvian embassy in Havana, killing a Cuban guard in the process. The Cubans were desperately seeking asylum, a form of diplomatic protection and safe passage out of a country that is granted to political refugees. When the Peruvian ambassador refused to hand over the asylum seekers to Cuban authorities, Castro's government reacted by removing its security force protecting the embassy. (It is a diplomatic tradition for host countries to provide guards for foreign embassies.) The strategy backfired. Within days, 10,000 Cubans squeezed onto the Peruvian embassy grounds, all seeking asylum.

Cuban officials agreed to allow the asylum seekers to leave the country. The government of Peru began airlifting Cubans out of the country. After two days, Castro announced that anyone who wanted to leave Cuba could go. To his surprise, thousands of Cubans packed into airports and port cities, including the port of Mariel, hoping to leave the country. President Jimmy Carter announced that the U.S. government would allow Cubans to settle in the United States: "Ours is a country of refugees. . . . We'll continue to provide an open heart and open arms to refugees seeking freedom from Communist domination."[5] Cuban Americans in Miami organized a flotilla of hundreds of small boats to go to Cuba to pick up relatives, friends, and even strangers. Taking advantage of the situation, Cuban officials decided to release prisoners and mental patients and place them on the boats headed to the United States. After four months, the United States ended the operation.

GOING IT ALONE

In the 1980s, as the revolutionary government attempted to maintain control over Cuba's economy and politics, it encountered a critical new problem. In 1983, Soviet officials informed Raúl Castro that they could no longer honor the security arrangement between the two countries. The Soviets would continue to provide weapons but would not defend the island against external threats. Without its Soviet defenders, the Cuban government had to provide its own security. Raúl began organizing a people's army to defend Cuba against a potential U.S. attack.

As economic conditions deteriorated in the Soviet Union, Soviet economic support to Cuba also began to shrink. To make up for the lack of financial assistance that the Soviets had provided for more than two decades, Castro announced a new economic program in 1986. The government would assume even greater control over the nation's economy and also boost domestic food production to make up for the loss of food imports from the Soviet Union and Eastern Europe.

In 1989, Soviet leader Mikhail Gorbachev came to Havana on an official visit. At home, he was pursuing several new groundbreaking reform programs, including a policy of government openness (known as *glasnost*) and economic restructuring (known as *perestroika*). Gorbachev was also working to forge a peaceful relationship with the United States. In private meetings with Castro and his advisers, the Soviet leader

Fidel Castro shakes hands with Soviet leader Mikhail Gorbachev during Gorbachev's visit to Cuba in April 1989. Following the collapse of the Soviet Union in 1991, Cuba found itself without a major international partner for the first time in decades.

informed the Cuban leadership that all Soviet economic and financial assistance would soon end. Shortly thereafter, an attempt to overthrow Gorbachev by hard-line elements in the Soviet government resulted in the collapse of the Soviet Union in 1991. Cuba had lost its longtime benefactor.

The Cuban government quickly introduced austerity programs to deal with the economic crisis caused by the Soviet collapse. More than 80 percent of the country's trade, including vital food imports, had been conducted with the Soviets. During what the government called "the Special Period," it introduced food rationing programs, encouraged Cubans to plant gardens, and instituted other measures to deal with severe shortages. Most Cubans struggled to survive. With reports of growing discontent coming out of Cuba, many Cuban exiles believed that the Cuban Revolution was approaching its end.

RELATIONS WITH THE UNITED STATES

Since the Cuban Missile Crisis of 1962, Cuba's relationship with the United States had fluctuated over the years. In 1975, the Cuban government held secret negotiations with the United States in which it signaled its willingness to compensate U.S. companies and citizens who lost property in Cuba's nationalization program in exchange for the United States ending the embargo. Cuba's military intervention in Angola, however, ended the discussions. Two years later, the Carter administration sought to improve relations with Cuba. Internal disagreements within the administration, however, undermined its efforts to reach any agreements. Tensions between the two countries increased during the Reagan administration. President Ronald Reagan included Cuba in many of his anti-Communist speeches. His administration also funded Radio Martí, a radio station that began beaming anti-Castro broadcasts to Cuba in 1985.

In the 1990s, the United States continued to exert pressure on the Cuban government. Congress passed the Helms-Burton Act in 1996, which widened U.S. economic sanctions against Cuba and allowed U.S. citizens to sue foreign companies that traded with Cuba to seek compensation for property nationalized by Cuba at the beginning of the Cuban Revolution. The law also specifically stated that the embargo would end only when a government that "does not include Fidel Castro or Raúl Castro" is in power.[6] The act had been passed in response to the Cuban Air Force shooting down two U.S. civilian planes piloted by members of Brothers to the Rescue, a group long opposed to Cuba's revolutionary government. The two planes had just dropped anti-revolution leaflets over Havana when they were shot down. The Cuban government disputed the Brothers' claim that their aircraft had been flying over international waters when shot down. The downing was not the last brutal suppression of dissidents. More recently, in 2003, the Cuban government jailed 75 political opponents, leading the United Nations' Human Rights Commission to censure the country.

RECENT YEARS

Throughout the decades since the start of the Cuban Revolution, Fidel Castro maintained a tight grip on his nation. Yet even that has changed recently. In July 2006, after Castro underwent gastric surgery, he handed temporary control of the government over to Raúl. He remained out of public sight for months, fueling rumors that he was dying. In February 2008, after Fidel announced his retirement, Raúl took over as president and began to implement some modest reforms, such as allowing everyday Cubans to purchase cell phones, DVD players, computers, and other items that were outlawed under Fidel Castro's government. He has also given merit pay to public employees and allowed the purchase of some government land by private farmers.

In April 2011, Fidel Castro resigned as first secretary of the Cuban Communist Party. He had led the party since 1965. Party members elected Raúl Castro as his successor. In one of its first actions under Raúl's leadership, the party voted to allow Cubans to buy and sell private property. Cuban law only allows Cubans to pass their homes to heirs or swap their homes with others. The party also recommended changing the terms of top political positions, limiting officeholders to two five-year terms. Raúl Castro cautioned that these reforms, along with others endorsed by the party, could take several years to enact.

The Impact of the Cuban Revolution

The Cuban Revolution was a watershed moment in the history of the twentieth century. It brought about profound changes in the lives of all Cubans and also had a significant impact on events throughout Latin America and in the United States, Europe, and Africa. At home, the revolution succeeded in its two basic goals: ousting the Batista regime and overturning the old political, economic, and social order that had stymied Cuba's development since its colonial days. Abroad, the Cuban revolutionaries also immediately sought political and economic independence from the United States, which had greatly influenced Cuba for 60 years. Seeking to break the economic hold that the United States had on Cuban politics and commerce, the Cuban government soon nationalized land and businesses owned by U.S. companies and citizens. It seized sugar plantations, cattle ranches, electric and telephone companies, banks, and other businesses, giving their owners only a promise to compensate their losses over time.

Unlike many previous Cuban governments, the revolutionary government has foiled all attempts to overthrow it. The Rebel Army and local militias defended Cuba from the threats posed by exile groups, many of which were supported by the United States. By thwarting the Bay of Pigs invasion and other attacks, the revolutionary government showed that it would endure. By allying itself with the Soviet Union, the government neutralized U.S. plots to topple the revolution.

Perhaps the Cuban Revolution's greatest success has come through creating social programs that help average Cubans. Its first major reform effort was a nationwide literacy campaign that quickly taught tens of thousands of Cubans to read. The government has continued to provide substantial funding for education. In a 2003 speech, Raúl Castro summarized the revolution's successes in education, claiming:

> [Cuba] has brought free education to 100% of the country's children. It has the highest school retention rate—over 99% between kindergarten and ninth grade—of all of the nations in the hemisphere. Its elementary school students rank first worldwide in the knowledge of their mother language and mathematics. The country also ranks first worldwide with the highest number of teachers per capita and the lowest number of students per classroom. . . . All citizens have the possibility of undertaking studies that will take them from kindergarten to a doctoral degree without spending a penny. Today, the country has 30 university graduates, intellectuals and professional artists for every one there was before the Revolution.[1]

The government has also made health care a priority. Indicators of the overall health of the Cuban population showed significant progress since the first year of the Cuban

Revolution. Infant mortality dropped from 6 percent in 1959 to 0.58 percent in 2009. (By comparison, the U.S. infant mortality rate in 2009 stood at 0.62 percent.) Between 1959 and 2009, life expectancy in Cuba increased by 15 years. Moreover, Cuba has received international praise for sending its special medical-response units to help nations around the globe when natural disasters strike.

The revolution's efforts to increase social justice included assuring racial, gender, and class equality. The government guaranteed black Cubans equal access to housing, government services, and employment opportunities and removed legal and cultural barriers that had prevented women from enjoying the same rights and opportunities as men. Today, women make up nearly two-thirds of Cuba's technical and scientific workforce.

The revolution has also achieved some successes in lifting poor Cubans out of poverty. Its educational campaigns gave people better jobs skills and its Agrarian Reform Law gave poor Cubans in rural areas land to grow their own crops.

THE REVOLUTION'S FAILURES

On the other hand, the Cuban Revolution's achievements in transforming Cuba into a socialist nation have come at a price. The Cuban government has not been able to shift from an agricultural-based economy to an industrialized economy. The revolutionaries had promised to end Cuba's reliance on the sugar industry, but they were unable to fulfill that promise. As a result of the U.S. embargo, the Cuban government made trade agreements to supply the Soviet Union and other Communist nations with sugar. The government instead focused its resources back into producing sugar, the country's major cash crop. Proceeds from sugar production enabled the government to pay for the discounted food and fuel that the Soviets shipped to Cuba.

In the years since the embargo was implemented, the government has claimed that it prevented Cuba's socialist experiment from reaching its full potential. In fact, the embargo provided the government with a handy excuse for all its failings. Cuban officials connected every political, economic, or social problem to Cuba's never-ending struggle against U.S. imperialism. It blamed the embargo for food shortages, for the lack of consumer goods, and for economic downturns. Critics of the revolution, however, blamed Cuba's economic woes on Castro's dictatorial rule and the government's socialist programs and policies. After the breakup of the Soviet Union, Cuba's economy limped along, especially whenever a hurricane destroyed sugar crops. Today, the Cuban economy relies mostly on tourism and on money sent to Cubans from relatives abroad.

The revolution also failed to keep its promise to restore civil rights guaranteed by the 1940 constitution and to hold fair elections. During the fight against the Batista regime, Castro and the M-26-7 praised democratic ideals. Once in power, however, they adopted a one-party political system and outlawed opposing political groups. The government denied basic civil liberties; censored newspapers, television broadcasts, and other media outlets; jailed artists, authors, and political dissenters on trumped-up charges. Although they provided opportunities for the masses, the forced equalities of the revolution stunted the personal development of individual Cubans.

The Cuban government reacted to attacks by antigovernment forces by creating a large national security operation, modeled on security systems in the Soviet Union and the Communist countries of Eastern Europe. Real and imagined threats were always present, creating a society always on alert for an attack. Today, a secret police force monitors Cubans, watching for any counterrevolutionary activity or comment. Neighbors spy on neighbors.

That said, the government's security concerns have some merit. It has real enemies, particularly among Cuban exile groups in Florida. Some of these groups are motivated, well

While the Cuban Revolution has had many successes, its two greatest failings have been its inability to provide more political freedom and greater economic opportunities to average Cubans.

funded, and politically powerful. Cuba continues to find itself in the unique position of being threatened by a large, powerful exile group, supported by a powerful nation that is located only about 200 miles (322 kilometers) from its capital city. In a sad irony, the Cuban government uses many of same repressive measures as did the Batista regime in order to identify internal opponents.

With the exception of Angola, the Cuban government's efforts to export its revolutionary model to Latin America and to Africa have failed. But perhaps its greatest failure has been its inability to keep Cubans from leaving their homeland. Since 1959, more than one million people have emigrated from

Cuba. The small number of Batista supporters and wealthy Cubans who fled in the early days of the revolution had little impact on the country. Cuba's revolution was severely harmed, however, when tens of thousands of Cubans left the country in later waves of emigration. Many Cubans had expected that the government that took control after the Batista regime would reinstate the constitution and adopt modest political reforms. They also assumed that it would maintain Cuba's democratic and free-market traditions. When the revolutionary government began steering the country in a radical new direction, many Cubans were shocked. When the government began seizing land, foreign companies, and domestic businesses, Cubans had to decide whether to commit themselves and their children to the revolution or to leave their homes and seek new lives elsewhere.

Economic and political concerns motivated many Cubans to leave the country in the early 1960s. Doctors, college professors, and other professionals saw no future for themselves in the country. When the government started jailing Cubans who disagreed with it, even those who supported the revolution began to flee. The Cuban Revolution also divided many families. Parents sent their children to the United States, expecting to be reunited soon. Emigrants left behind relatives, hoping to see them in the future. Everyone assumed that the revolution would collapse, as most Cuban governments before it had. Some of the separations became permanent.

LOOKING BACK AND LOOKING AHEAD

On January 1, 2009, Cuba celebrated the fiftieth anniversary of the Cuban Revolution. Raúl Castro gave a speech from the same balcony in Santiago where his brother Fidel had once proclaimed victory over Batista. While honoring those who died for the revolution, he urged his fellow Cubans to continue their resistance against the United States and thanked them for their sacrifices over the years:

One way or another, with more or less aggressiveness, every U.S. administration has tried to impose a regime change in Cuba. Resistance has been the key word and the explanation of every one of our victories throughout this half century of continued fighting when we have consistently acted on our own and taken our own risks. . . . For many years, Cuban revolutionaries have abided by Martí's [observation]: "Freedom is most precious and one must either accept to live without it or be determined to buy it for its price."[2]

He concluded by telling the audience, "Today, the Revolution is stronger than ever; it has never failed to stand by its principles, not even in the most difficult circumstances."[3]

Across the Straits of Florida, the anniversary caused sorrow in Miami, home to many Cuban exiles and their families. Ninoska Perez, a talk radio host and anti-Castro activist, told a reporter, "There's nothing to celebrate. All the revolution has brought is destruction to Cuba."[4] She had left Cuba as a young girl when her family fled. José Basulto, head of the counter-revolutionary Brothers to the Rescue group, called the revolution "a tragic event."[5]

The Cuban Revolution has endured for more than five decades. It has survived the Bay of Pigs, the Missile Crisis, and the relentless opposition of anti-revolution exiles in the United States. It has continued despite the U.S. embargo. It kept going after the loss of military and economic aid from the Soviet Union, its longtime benefactor. It has outlasted 10 U.S. presidents.

The remaining question is: Can it survive the death of the Castro brothers? What will happen once the eldery brothers are gone? Will the younger generation carry on the revolution? Will Cubans adopt a free-market economic system while maintaining one-party rule, as have the governments of China and Vietnam? Or will Cubans rise up to topple the government, following the example of democratic uprisings that ended

Cuban students take part in a ceremony in Havana to commemorate the fiftieth anniversary of the Cuban Revolution in October 2009. What the revolution will mean for this next generation of Cubans has yet to be determined.

Communist rule in Eastern Europe and dictatorships in the Middle East? Will the U.S. government continue its embargo, which has brought misery to millions of Cubans while failing in its goal to produce a regime change? Would it involve itself in an attempt to overthrow the Cuban government?

When asked by an interviewer in 2005 whether the Cuban Revolution would continue, Fidel Castro asserted, "The Revolution is based on principles. And the ideas that we defend have been, for quite some time, ideas shared by the entire nation."[6] When the interviewer also asked whether the revolution had succeeded, Castro answered, "What we've achieved is far greater than the dreams we could conceive back then, and we were pretty good dreamers."[7] Perhaps Castro made his most insightful comment about the Cuban Revolution nearly five decades earlier when he told Cubans, "Let us not fool ourselves into believing that the future will be easy; perhaps everything will be more difficult in the future."[8] The struggle for Cuba's future continues.

CHRONOLOGY

1492	Columbus lands in Cuba and claims the island for Spain.
1514	Spain builds its first settlements in Cuba.
1522	First African slaves arrive in Cuba.
1868-1878	Rebels clash with colonial forces in first war of independence.
1895	José Martí is killed.
1895-1898	Rebels fail to overthrow colonial authorities in second war of independence.

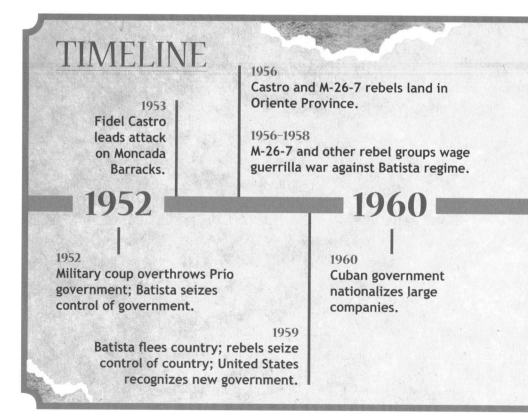

TIMELINE

1953
Fidel Castro leads attack on Moncada Barracks.

1956
Castro and M-26-7 rebels land in Oriente Province.

1956–1958
M-26-7 and other rebel groups wage guerrilla war against Batista regime.

1952

1960

1952
Military coup overthrows Prío government; Batista seizes control of government.

1960
Cuban government nationalizes large companies.

1959
Batista flees country; rebels seize control of country; United States recognizes new government.

1898   U.S. defeats Spain in the Spanish-American War; Spain cedes all rights to Cuba to United States.

1898-1902   U.S. military occupies Cuba.

1902   Cuba gains independence; Tomás Estrada serves as nation's first president; Platt Amendment goes into force.

1933   Sergeants' Rebellion overthrows Céspedes government.

1940   Second Cuban constitution is adopted.

1952   Military coup overthrows Prío government; Fulgencio Batista seizes control of government.

1953   Fidel Castro leads attack on Moncada Barracks.

1956   Castro and M-26-7 rebels land in Oriente Province.

1962
United States adopts trade embargo of Cuba; Cuba becomes Soviet ally; Cuban Missile Crisis occurs in October.

1991
Soviet aid to Cuba ends when Soviet Union breaks into separate nations.

2008
Fidel Castro resigns; Raúl Castro assumes control of Cuban government.

1961

2009

1961
Cuban forces thwart U.S.-sponsored Bay of Pigs invasion.

2009
Cuba celebrates the fiftieth anniversary of the Cuban Revolution.

1968
Castro reorganizes government; Communist Party of Cuba in control of one-party government.

1980
More than 100,000 Cubans leave Cuba during Mariel boatlift.

1956-1958	M-26-7 and other rebel groups wage guerrilla war against Batista regime.
1959	Batista flees country; rebels seize control of country; United States recognizes new government.
1960	Cuban government nationalizes large companies.
1961	Cuban forces thwart U.S.-sponsored Bay of Pigs invasion.
1962	United States adopts trade embargo of Cuba; Cuba becomes Soviet ally; Cuban Missile Crisis occurs in October.
1968	Castro reorganizes government; Communist Party of Cuba is in control of one-party government; Cuban government nationalizes smaller companies.
1970	Ten-million-ton sugar harvest initiative fails.
1972	Cuba joins Comecon.
1975	Cuba sends troops to Angola.
1980	More than 100,000 Cubans leave Cuba during Mariel boatlift.
1991	Soviet aid to Cuba ends when Soviet Union breaks into separate nations.
1996	U.S. Congress passes Helms-Burton Act.
1998	Pope John Paul II visits Cuba.
2008	Fidel Castro resigns as president of Cuba; Raúl Castro assumes control of Cuban government.
2009	Cuba celebrates the fiftieth anniversary of the Cuban Revolution.
2011	Fidel Castro steps down as head of the Cuban Communist Party; Raúl Castro is named as his successor.

NOTES

CHAPTER 1

1. John Dorschner. "Fidel Castro: The Last Time." *Miami Herald*. http://www.miamiherald.com/multimedia/news/castro/batista.html.

2. Volker Skierka, *Fidel Castro: A Biography*. New York: Wiley-Blackwell, 2004, p. 68.

3. Herbert L. Matthews, "Castro Decrees a Halt in Strike Paralyzing Cuba," *New York Times*, January 5, 1959, p. 1.

4. R. Hart Phillips, "Castro Regrets Delay in Arrival," *New York Times*, January 5, 1959, p. 3.

5. Fidel Castro. "Camp Columbia Speech," January 9, 1959. Latin America Network Information Center. http://lanic.utexas.edu/project/castro.

6. Ibid.

7. R. Hart Phillips, *Cuba: Island of Paradox*. New York: McDowell, Obolensky, 1959, p. 406.

8. R. Hart Phillips, "Havana Welcomes Castro at End of Triumphal Trip," *New York Times*, January 9, 1959, p. 9.

9. Ibid.

CHAPTER 2

1. Quoted in Richard Gott, *Cuba: A New History*. New Haven, Conn.: Yale University Press, 2004, p. 13.

2. Henry Kamen, *How Spain Became a World Power, 1492–1763*. New York: HarperCollins, 2003, p. 493.

3. Rex Hudson, ed., *In Cuba: A Country Study*, 4th ed. Washington, D.C.: Federal Research Division, Library of Congress, 2002, p. 47.

4. José M. Hernández, *Cuba and the United States: Intervention and Militarism, 1868–1933*. Austin: University of Texas Press, 1993, p. 73.

5. Samuel Farber, *The Origins of the Cuban Revolution Reconsidered*. Chapel Hill: University of North Carolina Press, 2006, p. 71.

CHAPTER 3

1. Quoted in Hugh Thomas, *The Cuban Revolution*. New York: HarperCollins, 1986, p. 784.

2. Ibid.

3. Quoted in PBS, *The American Experience: Fidel Castro*. PBS.org. http://www.pbs.org/wgbh/amex/castro/peopleevents.

4. Gott, *Cuba*, p. 152.

5. Jon Lee Anderson, *Che Guevara: A Revolutionary Life*. New York: Grove, 1997, p. 175.

6. Robert Quirk, *Fidel Castro*. New York: Norton, 1995, p. 141.

7. Herbert L. Matthews, "Cuban Rebel Is Visited in Hideout," *New York Times*, February 24, 1957, p. 1.

8. Ibid., p. 4.

9. Ibid., p. 1.

10. Che Guevara, *Reminiscences of the Cuban Revolutionary War*. New York: Ocean, 2006, p. 85.

CHAPTER 4

1. Homer Bigart, "Castro, in Interview, Demands Army's Departure from Oriente Province, Then Election Supervised by O.A.S," *New York Times*, February 25, 1958, p. 1.
2. Tad Szulc, *Fidel: A Critical Portrait*. New York: HarperCollins, 2000, p. 439.
3. Thomas, *The Cuban Revolution*, p. 210.
4. Ibid., p. 217.
5. Hugh Thomas, *Cuba, or the Pursuit of Freedom*. New York: Da Capo, 1998, p. 1001.
6. Ibid., p. 1019.
7. Ramón L. Bonachea and Marta San Martín, *The Cuban Insurrection, 1952–1959*. New York: Transaction, 1974, p. 312.

CHAPTER 5

1. Gott, *Cuba*, p. 168.
2. R. Hart Phillips, "Military Court in Cuba Dooms 14 for 'War Crimes,'" *New York Times*, January 13, 1959, p.1, 12.
3. Quoted in Lars Schoultz, *That Infernal Little Cuban Republic: The United States and the Cuban Revolution*. Chapel Hill: University of North Carolina Press, 2009, p. 93.
4. Ibid., p. 92.
5. Philip Benjamin, "City Gives Castro a Noisy Greeting," *New York Times*, April 22, 1959, pp. 1, 14.
6. Ibid.
7. Fidel Castro. "On the Promulgation of the Agrarian Law," May 17, 1959. Latin America Network Information Center. http://lanic.utexas.edu/project/castro.
8. Gott, *Cuba*, p. 180.

CHAPTER 6

1. Gott, *Cuba*, p. 184.
2. Ibid., p. 193.
3. Ibid., p. 195.
4. Ernest R. May and Philip Zelikow, eds., *The Kennedy Tapes: Inside the White House During the Cuban Missile Crisis*. New York: Norton, 2002, p. 184.
5. Ibid., p. 185.
6. Ibid.
7. Ibid., p. 186.
8. Ibid.
9. Gott, *Cuba*, p. 201.
10. John F. Kennedy, Press Conference 45, November 20, 1962. JFKLibrary.org. http://www.jfklibrary.org.

CHAPTER 7

1. Gott, *Cuba*, p. 215.
2. Fidel Castro, "The Second Declaration of Havana," February 4, 1962. Walterlippmann.com. http://www.walterlippmann.com/fc-02-04-1962.html.
3. Gott, *Cuba*, p. 223.
4. Fidel Castro. Speech at the Inaugural Session of the Cuban National Assembly, December 2, 1976. Latin America Network Information Center. http://.lanic.utexas.edu/project/castro/db/1976/19761202.html.
5. Gott, *Cuba*, p. 268.

6. Cuban Liberty and Democratic Solidarity (Libertad) Act of 1996, Section 205(C)(7). Treasury.gov. http://www.treasury.gov.

CHAPTER 8

1. Raúl Castro. Speech at the May Day Event, May 1, 2003. Marxists.org. http://www.marxists.org/history/cuba/archive/castro/2003/05/01.htm.

2. Raúl Castro. Speech on the 50th Anniversary of the Revolution, January 1, 2009. http://embacuba.cubaminrex.cu/Default.aspx?tabid=9536.

3. Ibid.

4. Jeff Franks. "Cuba Marks 50th Anniversary of Castro Revolution," January 1, 2009. Reuters. http://uk.reuters.com/article/2009/01/01/us-cuba-revolution-idUKTRE4BM3A520090101.

5. Ibid.

6. Fidel Castro and Igancio Ramonet, *Fidel Castro: My Life*. New York: Scribner, 2006, p. 622.

7. Ibid., p. 583.

8. Fidel Castro. "Camp Columbia Speech," January 9, 1959. Latin America Network Information Center. http://lanic.utexas.edu/project/castro.

BIBLIOGRAPHY

Anderson, Jon Lee. *Che Guevara: A Revolutionary Life*. New York: Grove, 1997.

Argote-Freyre, Frank. *Fulgencio Batista: From Revolutionary to Strongman*. New Brunswick, N.J.: Rutgers University Press, 2006.

Benjamin, Philip. "City Gives Castro a Noisy Greeting." *New York Times*, April 22, 1959.

Bigart, Homer. "Castro, in Interview, Demands Army's Departure from Oriente Province, Then Election Supervised by O.A.S." *New York Times*, February 25, 1958.

Bonachea, Ramón L., and Marta San Martín. *The Cuban Insurrection, 1952–1959*. New York: Transaction, 1974.

Castro, Fidel. "Camp Columbia Speech." January 9, 1959. Available online. URL: http:// lanic.utexas.edu/project/castro.

———. *Che: A Memoir*. New York: Ocean, 2005.

———. "On the Promulgation of the Agrarian Law." May 17, 1959. Available online. URL: http://lanic.utexas.edu/project/castro.

———. "The Second Declaration of Havana." February 4, 1962. Available online. URL: http://www.walterlippmann.com/fc-02-04-1962.html.

———. Speech at the Inaugural Session of the Cuban National Assembly. December 2, 1976. Available online. URL: http://lanic.utexas.edu/project/castro/db/1976/19761202.html.

Castro, Fidel, and Ignacio Ramonet. *Fidel Castro: My Life*. New York: Scribner, 2006.

Castro, Raúl. Speech at the May Day Event. May 1, 2003. Available online. URL: http://www.marxists.org/history/cuba/archive/castro/2003/05/01.htm.

————. Speech on the 50th Anniversary of the Revolution. January 1, 2009. Available online. URL: http://embacuba .cubaminrex.eu/Default.aspx?tabid=9536.

Cuban Liberty and Democratic Solidarity (Libertad) Act of 1996. Section 205(C)(7). Available online. URL: http://www.treasury .gov/resource-center/sanctions/Documents/libertad.pdf.

Dorschner, John. "Fidel Castro: The Last Time." *Miami Herald*. Available online. URL: http://www.miamiherald.com/multi media/news/castro/batista.html.

English, T.J. *Havana Nocturne: How the Mob Owned Cuba . . . and Then Lost It to the Revolution*. New York: HarperCollins, 2008.

Farber, Samuel. *The Origins of the Cuban Revolution Reconsidered*. Chapel Hill: University of North Carolina Press, 2006.

Franks. Jeff. "Cuba Marks 50th Anniversary of Castro Revolution." Reuters, January 1, 2009. Available online. URL: http://uk.reuters.com/article/2009/01/01/us-cuba-revolution -idUKTRE4BM3A520090101.

Gott, Richard. *Cuba: A New History*. New Haven, Conn.: Yale University Press, 2004.

Guevara, Che. *Reminiscences of the Cuban Revolutionary War*. New York: Ocean, 2006.

Hernández, José M. *Cuba and the United States: Intervention and Militarism, 1868–1933*. Austin: University of Texas Press, 1993.

Hudson, Rex, ed. *In Cuba: A Country Study*, 4th ed. Washington, D.C.: Federal Research Division, Library of Congress, 2002.

Kamen, Henry. *How Spain Became a World Power, 1492–1763*. New York: HarperCollins, 2003.

Kennedy, John F. Press Conference 45. November 20, 1962. Available online. URL: http://www.jfklibrary.org/Research/

Ready-Reference/Press-Conferences/News-Conference-45. aspx.

Maclean, Betsy. *Rebel Lives: Haydée Santamaría*. New York: Ocean Press, 2003.

Matthews, Herbert L. "Castro Decrees a Halt in Strike Paralyzing Cuba." *New York Times*, January 5, 1959, p. 1.

———. "Cuban Rebel Is Visited in Hideout." *New York Times*, February 24, 1957.

May, Ernest R. and Philip Zelikow, eds. *The Kennedy Tapes: Inside the White House During the Cuban Missile Crisis*. New York: Norton, 2002.

PBS. *The American Experience: Fidel Castro*. Available online. URL: http://www.pbs.org/wgbh/amex/castro.

Phillips, R. Hart. "Havana Welcomes Castro at End of Triumphant Trip." *New York Times*, January 9, 1959.

———. "Military Courts in Cuba Dooms 14 for 'War Crimes.'" *New York Times*, January 9, 1959.

———. "Castro Regrets Delay in Arrival." *New York Times*, January 5, 1959.

———. *Cuba: Island of Paradox*. New York: McDowell, Obolensky, 1959.

Quirk, Robert. *Fidel Castro*. New York: Norton, 1995.

Schoultz, Lars. *That Infernal Little Cuban Republic: The United States and the Cuban Revolution*. Chapel Hill: University of North Carolina Press, 2009.

Skierka, Volker. *Fidel Castro: A Biography*. New York: Wiley-Blackwell, 2004.

Sweig, Julia E. *Cuba: What Everyone Should Know*. New York: Oxford University Press, 2009.

Szulc, Tad. "Clues to the Enigma Called Castro." *New York Times Magazine*, December 9, 1962.

———. *Fidel: A Critical Portrait.* New York: HarperCollins, 2000.

Thomas, Hugh. *Cuba, or the Pursuit of Freedom.* New York: Da Capo, 1998.

———. *The Cuban Revolution.* New York: HarperCollins, 1986.

FURTHER RESOURCES

BOOKS

Castro, Fidel, and Ignacio Ramonet. *Fidel Castro: My Life*. New York: Scribner, 2006.

Cox, Vicki. *Fidel Castro*. New York: Chelsea House, 2003.

Crompton, Samuel Willard. *The Sinking of the USS Maine: Declaring War Against Spain*. New York: Chelsea House, 2008.

Crooker, Richard A., and Zoran Pavlovic. *Cuba*. New York: Chelsea House, 2010.

Dunn, John M. *Life in Castro's Cuba*. San Diego: Lucent, 2004.

Francis, Amy. *The U.S. Policy on Cuba*. Detroit: Greenhaven, 2009.

Gay, Kathlyn. *Leaving Cuba: From Operation Pedro Pan to Elian*. Brookfield, Conn.: Twenty-First Century, 2000.

Golay, Michael. *Spanish-American War*. New York: Chelsea House, 2003.

Leonard, Thomas M. *Castro and the Cuban Revolution*. Westport, Conn.: Greenwood, 1999.

———. *Fidel Castro*. Westport, Conn.: Greenwood, 2004.

McConnell, William S., ed. *Living Through the Cuban Missile Crisis*. San Diego: Greenhaven, 2006.

Sterngass, Jon. *José Martí*. New York: Chelsea House, 2006.

Uschan, Michael V. *Che Guevara: Revolutionary*. Farmington Hills, Mich.: Lucent, 2007.

WEB SITES

The Art History Archive: Alberto Korda
http://www.arthistoryarchive.com/arthistory/photography/Alberto-Korda.html

Fidel Castro: Times Coverage, 1957–1959
  http://www.nytimes.com/ref/world/americas/CASTRO_
  ARCHIVE.html

Latin American Network Information Center: Castro Speech
  Database
  http://lanic.utexas.edu/la/cb/cuba/castro.html

University of Miami's Institute for Cuban and Cuban-
  American Studies: Cuba On-line
  http://cuba.iccas.miami.edu.

PICTURE CREDITS

INDEX

ABOUT THE AUTHOR

G.S. PRENTZAS is the author of more than 25 books for young readers. He wrote *The Marshall Plan* in Chelsea House's MILE-STONES IN MODERN WORLD HISTORY series and *The World Health Organization* in Chelsea House's GLOBAL ORGANIZA-TIONS series. He lives near New York City.

He dedicates this book to Chad Bowen and Michelle Rivas, for all the good times at El Rancho.